WOMANIST
AND
FEMINIST
AESTHETICS

WOMANIST AND FEMINIST AESTHETICS

A Comparative Review

Tuzyline Jita Allan

OHIO UNIVERSITY PRESS
ATHENS

Ohio University Press, Athens, Ohio 45701
© 1995 by Tuzyline Jita Allan
Printed in the United States of America
All rights reserved
Ohio University Press books are printed on acid-free paper ∞

99 98 97 96 95   5 4 3 2 1 (CLOTH)
01 00 99 98 97 96   5 4 3 2 1 (PBK)

Library of Congress Cataloging-in-Publication Data

Allan, Tuzyline Jita.
    Womanist and feminist aesthetics : a comparative review / Tuzyline
Jita Allan.
        p.   cm.
    Includes bibliographical references and index.
    ISBN 0-8214-1109-8 (CL)   ISBN 0-8214-1152-7 (PBK)
    1. English fiction—Women authors—History and criticism.
2. English fiction—20th century—History and criticism.
3. Feminism and literature—History—20th century.   4. Women and
literature—History—20th century.   5. Woolf, Virginia, 1882-1941.
Mrs. Dalloway.   6. Drabble, Margaret, 1939-   Middle ground.
7. Walker, Alice, 1944-   Color purple.   8. Emecheta, Buchi. Joys
of motherhood.   9. Aesthetics, Modern—20th century.   I. Title.
PR888.F45A45   1995
823'.91099287—dc20
                                                        94-45726
                                                            CIP

In Memoriam

For my parents—my father, Joseph Konchekma Younge, who told me at the tender age of seven, "Make your books your friends," and my mother, Lillian "Sunbeam" Alaba, who taught me by example that to live is to love.

Contents

Acknowledgments   ix

Introduction   1

1

Mrs. Dalloway: A Study of
Woolf's Social Ambivalence   19

2

The Middle Ground: Determinism in a
a Changing World   45

3

The Color Purple: A Study of
Walker's Womanist Gospel   69

4

The Joys of Motherhood: A Study of
a Problematic Womanist Aesthetic   95

Conclusion   118

Notes   122

Bibliography   137

Acknowledgments

I am indebted professionally and personally to many people for this project. First, I wish to thank almost two generations of black and white feminist critics of second-wave twentieth-century feminism for opening up and broadening new vistas of reading literature. Their critical energy and devotion to women's texts has been nothing short of phenomenal. They are too numerous to name here, but my text and bibliography capture a sense of their invaluable contributions. I am also grateful to a number of African feminist critics: Filomena Chioma Steady, Molara Ogundipe-Leslie, Chikwenye Okonjo Ogunyemi, Carol Boyce Davies, Ann Adams, Margaret Bushby, Marie Umeh, Brenda Berrian, Mildred Hill-Lubin, Abena Busia, Elizabeth Mudimbe-Boyi, Obioma Nnaemeka, Lloyd Brown, Charlotte Bruner, Eileen Julien, Arlene Elder, to name a few, committed scholars and critics, who have pushed the limits of African literary discourse to make room for women writers such as Flora Nwapa, Ama Ata Aidoo, Bessie Head, Buchi Emecheta, Mariama Bâ, Aminatu Sow Fall, Tsitsi Dangarembga, Werewere Liking, Rebecca Njau, and Grace Ogot.

I would like to express my deepest gratitude to Susan Squier for nourishing my early thinking on this project and keeping a watchful eye on its development; to Rose Zimbardo, whose passion for teaching is equalled only by her devotion to her students; to Sallie Sears, a consummate reader of texts and a truly fine teacher; and to Helen Cooper for her interest in this work.

I want to give special thanks to the Northeastern Modern Language Association (NEMLA) Book Award Committee, especially Dr. Charlotte Goodman, for finding merit in this project. To Professors Regina Jennings and Elaine Delancey, perceptive and constructive readers both, I express profound gratitude.

To my editor, Duane Schneider, and the editorial staff at Ohio University Press, especially Holly Panich, Helen Gawthrop, Sharon Arnold, and Nancy Basmajian, I extend heartfelt thanks for their patience and unfailing support.

For administrative support in the form of released time from Baruch College I wish to thank Dean Norman Feinstein.

Finally, I would like to acknowledge my debt to my family and friends for providing emotional support and the intellectual stimulation necessary to see this project through: Hawa Allan, Marilyn Zucker, Mary DeSena, Tom Fink, and Barbara Kponou, my "sister" and typist.

Introduction

DECODING WOMANIST GRAMMAR
OF DIFFERENCE

Kate Millet's *Sexual Politics* marked a paradigmatic shift in American intellectual life from civil rights to women's rights.[1] The book appeared at a time when black and white women activists, alienated by the male-dominated center of the civil rights movement and the increasingly sexist tone of its revolutionary branch, were beginning to channel their energies into formidable resistance against women's social subordination.[2] *Sexual Politics* is a landmark in more than one sense. Most often acknowledged is the fact that it anticipated the theoretical and critical feminist discourse of the 1970s. Millet argued that the socialization of women into inferior beings had been replicated in the works of D. H. Lawrence, Norman Mailer, Henry Miller, and Jean Genet, an argument that laid the foundation for the two-pronged feminist enterprise of theoretical and critical investigation that has dominated academic inquiry for the past two decades.

As forerunner, *Sexual Politics* also initiated the practice of ethnocentrism within feminist studies. Educated, middle-class white women devised theories about middle-class white women and gave them a universal stamp, thereby erasing or invalidating the experiences of the majority of women, who were excluded from one or both of these categories.[3] Other critics soon challenged these theories and charged their exponents with ethnocentric arrogance and bias. Women's varied cultural, racial, class, and sexual identities, these critics argued, defied homogenization. Besides, what justification was there for positing a middle-class, Eurocentric model of womanhood as the female ideal? Were white feminists appropriating femaleness in the same way that white men had appropriated maleness? And if so, how different then was the feminist enterprise from those male practices of domination it was attempting to expose? Such an interrogation led to the determination that the early theoretical accounts of women's social roles mirrored the self/other dichotomy of phallocentric thought.[4]

Early feminist criticism thus proved just as exclusionary and controversial as the male social structures it decried. The critical project to unearth and reinstate women writers buried beneath age-long patriarchal neglect or scorn seemed to reenact, through its own neglect of nonwhite women, the very process it set out to correct. Critical reappraisals of the literature of Anglo-American women writers omitted or mentioned only cursorily black female writers. In the ensuing backlash, Alice Walker denounced both the practice and the practitioners, citing in her oft-quoted essay, "One's Child of One's Own," a particularly startling example of unbridled ethnocentrism:

> In the prologue to her book, *The Female Imagination*, Patricia Meyer Spacks attempts to explain why her book deals solely with women in the "Anglo-American literary tradition." (She means, of course, *white* women in the Anglo-American literary tradition. Speaking of the books she has chosen to study, she writes: "Almost all delineate the lives of white middle-class women. Phyllis Chesler has remarked,

'I have no theory to offer Third World female psychology in America. . . . As a white woman, I'm reluctant and unable to construct theories about experiences I haven't had.' So am I: the books I talk about *describe familiar experience, belong to a familiar cultural setting*. . . . My bibliography *balances works everyone knows (Jane Eyre, Middlemarch)* with works that should be better known (*The Story of Mary MacLane*). Still, the question remains: Why only these?"[5]

Spacks's paternalistic tone, universalizing rhetoric, and self-distancing from the Third World female "other" all replicate the masculinist performance of gendered discourse. To realize the full ideological import of her statement, one need simply replace *Jane Eyre, Middlemarch,* and *The Story of Mary MacLane* with, say, *Vanity Fair, The Mayor of Casterbridge,* and *Roderick Random,* respectively. The move reinvokes the hegemonic authority of male-directed canonic critical discourse and simultaneously implicates Spacks in a shared awareness of cultural power.

Barbara Smith referred to the hierarchization of racial gender within the new community of academic feminism as a "barely disguised cultural 'imperialism'" underwritten by resistance to the idea that "Black and female identity . . . coexist."[6] Walker concurred, linking the effort to crystallize white feminism into a normative femininity to white male appropriation of manhood:

It is, apparently, inconvenient, if not downright mind straining, for white women scholars to think of Black women as women, perhaps because "woman" (like "man" among white males) is a name they are claiming for themselves, and themselves alone. Racism decrees that if *they* are now women . . . then Black women must, perforce, be something else. (*Gardens* 376)

Black women's creativity at the beginning of the second wave of twentieth-century feminism also stood in the shadow of what Calvin Hernton would call a "mountain of sexism," a peak as formidable as its racial counterpart. Denounced variously by black feminist critics, "the legacy of male chauvinism in the black literary world" suffered a crushing defeat, ironically, at the hands of a male critic.[7] In the eponymous second chapter of *The Sexual Mountain and Black Women Writers* Hernton launched what Claudia Tate dubbed a "male womanist" attack against what he perceived as "feelings of envy, jealousy, resentment and paranoia on the part of the men" toward black women writers.[8] Hernton stacked up an impressive record of black women's literary production against a pattern of female devaluation within the male-dominated black literary establishment. The catalogue conveyed a sense of unbroken confrontation between black women and men, animated by what Tate called the latter's "phallocentric privilege."[9]

Hernton's essay assumes greater significance beyond marking a radical shift in priorities within the predominant African American critical tradition. It is explicit regarding the range and scope of black feminist insurgency, leaving no doubt as to the promise of vindication embodied in the emergent effort to unearth and reinstate black women's writing. This effort, responding to the concurrent systems of male and white female marginalization already described, began with the need to develop a parallel "historical tradition" located in the nexus of "specific political, social and economic experience" unique to black women.[10] The resulting scholarship has been both virtuosic and unrelenting. From Mary Helen Washington's modest but influential trilogy—*Black-Eyed Susans, Midnight Birds*, and *Invented Lives*—to the dazzling architectonics of Henry Louis Gates's Schomburg series, black women's narratives now lend an awesome presence to the American literary landscape, smothering the anxiety of displacement that marked their painful gestation.[11]

The development of black feminist criticism has been slower, though no less dramatic, perhaps because its parallel track bears disproportionately the strains and stresses of the project to rehabilitate black female creativity. The pressure points were evident from the start. Caught between white feminist and black male hegemonies, black feminist critics faced the difficult task of constructing a new identity in both cultures based on a dialectical relationship of cooperation and resistance. Deborah McDowell articulated well the dilemma in her founding essay, "New Directions for Black Feminist Criticism." Inegalitarian productions of femininity and blackness in mainstream feminist and African American discourses, she argued, called for an alternative, competing and un-self-limiting vision from black women. McDowell decried the "decidedly . . . practical" and idealistic tone of early black feminist analysis and challenged its practitioners to move beyond sloganeering and political isolationism to a theoretical level of discourse with ties to black male literature, white feminist criticism and "the critical methodology handed down by white men."[12]

In *Reconstructing Womanhood*, Hazel Carby collapsed the chronological configurations of black feminist criticism—from Barbara Smith's "Toward a Black Feminist Criticism" to Barbara Christian's *Black Feminist Criticism*—in an effort to foreground a historically sound basis for theorizing differences between black and white women. Carby shared McDowell's disdain for the idealistic strain in black feminist criticism but also indicted the whole feminist myth of "a lost [American] sisterhood" on similar grounds. The "boundaries that separate white feminists from all women of color" constitute a "history of difference" that, Carby insisted, cannot be ignored by contemporary feminists.[13] Her reading of this "cultural history" offers a powerful and exciting example of the critical sophistication McDowell advocated. More crucially, in terms of my own objectives in this book, Carby refigured black feminist criticism as "a problem, not a solution, as a sign that should be interrogated, a locus of contradictions."[14]

Standing on a discursive middle ground between McDowell's not-so-sanguine expectations and Carby's hearty historicization, Alice Walker's "womanist" ethos embodies both the frustration and the promise of black feminist criticism. Resolutely idealistic and essentialist, womanism reflects nonetheless a marked acceleration in black feminists' readiness to reframe the sexual debate around culturally specific differences between white women and women of color. Walker spells out her definition of "womanist" in four choral stanzas bearing the following excerpted content, which I have arranged according to thematic importance:

> Womanist: A black feminist or feminist of color. . . .
>
> > Usually referring to outrageous, audacious, courageous or *wilful* behavior. Wanting to know more and in greater depth than is considered "good" for one. . . .
> >
> > A woman who loves other women sexually and/or nonsexually. Appreciates and prefers women's culture, women's emotional flexibility . . . and women's strength. . . .
> >
> > Committed to survival and wholeness of entire people, male *and* female. Not a separatist. . . .
> >
> > Womanist is to feminist as purple is to lavender. (*Gardens*, xi–xii)

Even with the filter of metaphor, the last statement fails to conceal the deep lines of division drawn here between black and white feminists. Walker sets up (black) womanism and (white) feminism in a binary opposition from which the former emerges a privileged, original term and the latter, a devalued, pale replica. With this reversal of the existing paradigm of power relations, womanist consciousness becomes the strategic fulcrum of the project of female restoration. Walker intends the major themes of womanist epistemology— audacity, woman-centeredness, and whole(some)ness of vision—to be understood as critical imperatives in the effort to fashion a framework of feminist resistance to patriarchy. These themes will serve as both a structural and a guiding principle of this book, as I examine the merits of Walker's critique of and implicit challenge to white feminist praxis. But first it is helpful to determine the nature of the response to womanism's differentiated presence within feminism.

In the field of contesting attitudes toward womanism, approbation predominates. For many feminists of color, the concept is a rich source of cultural capital in a social economy weighted heavily against them. Consequently, womanism has helped to fortify the long-standing discontent over white feminists' appropriation of womanhood, prompting active rather than reactive forms of criticism. In "Womanism: The Dynamics of the Contemporary Black Female Novel in English," Nigerian-born critic Chikwenye Ogunyemi captures the new critical attitude in her opening sentence:

> What does a black woman novelist go through as she comes in contact with white feminist writing and realizes that Shakespeare's illustrious sisters belong to the second sex, a situation that has turned them into impotent eunuchs without rooms of their own in which to read and write their very own literature, so that they have become madwomen now emerging from the attic, determined to fight for their rights by engaging in the acrimonious politics of sex?[15]

This brilliant conflation of familiar Euro-American feminist themes and texts is a linguistic act that mocks white feminist narratives of victimization, narratives that have themselves, in their exclusivity, victimized nonwhite women. The satiric backdrop helps to illuminate the contrasting image of the womanist writer who "along with her consciousness of sexual issues . . . incorporate[s] racial, cultural, national, economic, and political considerations into her philosophy."[16] The goal of this many-sided vision, Ogunyemi argues, is a gender-free Pan-Africanism ("the unity of blacks everywhere under the enlightened control of men and women"), a far cry from the self-serving idea of a "separatist, idyllic existence away from . . . men's world" that preoccupies the white woman writer.[17]

Barbara Smith had already made the connection between womanism and race, culture, and politics in her introduction to *Home Girls: A Black Feminist Anthology*, published the same year as Walker's *In Search of Our Mothers' Gardens*. "I have always felt," Smith wrote, "that Black women's ability to function with dignity, independence, and imagination in the face of total adversity—that is, in the face of white America—points to an innate feminist potential." Like Walker, Smith locates this quality in the socializing black female ethic embodied in the injunction "Act like you have some sense." The ability to forge a "connection between plain common sense and a readiness to fight for change" bespeaks, for Smith, a culture-specific feminism deserving the distinction conferred by the term "womanist."[18]

What Patricia Hill Collins culls from womanism to assist in her mapping of the epistemological contours of black feminism is a "humanist vision" born out of black women's struggle against multiple oppressions. She posits the womanist idea of "commit[ment] to the survival and wholeness of entire people, male and female" as a recurrent theme among black women intellectuals, from Anna Julia Cooper to June Jordan. These women's "words and actions," according to Collins, "resonate with a strikingly similar theme of the oneness of all human life"—that is, with womanist intensity.[19] Collins thus shares with Ogunyemi and Smith a belief in womanism's culture-specific ability to re(ad)dress the wrongs of white feminist practice.

Africana Womanism: Reclaiming Ourselves, by Clenora Hudson-Weems, offers the first critique of Walker's womanism as it attempts to radically reconfigure the concept. Defined as "an ideology created and designed for all women of African descent," Africana womanism, as Hudson-Weems depicts it, is in full retreat from white feminism, and simultaneously rejects "Black feminism, African feminism, [and] Walker's womanism."[20] Hudson-Weems's charge of racism brought up against white feminists is familiar but no less vehement. Indeed, she forecloses all discussion on the subject based on the notion that white women's racist attitudes are immutable. This perspective underlies her critique of black and African feminisms which, she argues, are ideologically doomed by association with white feminism, summed up as "a sort of inverted White patriarchy, with the White feminist now in command and on top."[21] Walker's brand of womanism does not fare any better. Its flaw, according to Hudson-Weems, is in its single-minded focus on "the woman, her sexuality, and her culture,"[22] a clear marker of its kinship with white feminism. *Africana Womanism*, therefore, aims to promote a woman's project on grounds totally unaffiliated with Euro-American feminism and unannexed to black and African feminisms.

Hudson-Weems's womanism may help to explain why prominent black feminist critics have distanced themselves from Walker's womanist theory. Hudson-Weems openly expresses a separatist ideology that Walker only suggests. But, McDowell, Carby, and bell hooks, among others, firmly reject a separatist black feminist enterprise, direct or implicit. These critics are acutely aware of the racist ideologies underlining mainstream feminist praxis and have dueled fiercely with the practitioners. Yet they do not see a sustainable strategy in a separatist or essentialist paradigm of black female subjectivity such as embodied in womanism. Though Carby, for instance, makes no mention of the term in *Reconstructing Womanhood*, it is nonetheless implied in her critique of black feminist critics' "reliance on a common, or shared, experience" for the construction of theory.[23] Similarly, McDowell's warning that a "separatist position" could bring black feminist criticism perilously close to the paralyzing zone of "critical absolutism" both anticipates and undermines the womanist idea[24] bell hooks's disaffinity with the term, however, is somewhat ambiguous. While she questions its "commitment to struggle and change" and condemns its use as a sundering tool, she puts the blame for its misappropriation not on Walker but on womanist enthusiasts instead: "I hear black women academics laying claim to the term 'womanist' while rejecting 'feminist.' I do not think Alice Walker intended this term to deflect from feminist commitment."[25]

hooks's exoneration of Walker from womanist politics of division reveals a key dilemma "mainstream" black feminist critics face regarding womanism.[26] Refusing on the one hand to indulge its essentialist appetite, they are, on the other, loath to kick up dust around the subject in a way that might offset the healthy respect Walker commands within both black and white feminist circles. In two chapters in *Yearning*, for example, hooks conducts an astute critique of "the constricting notion of blackness" without any mention of womanism.[27] And in a third, she cites the much-rebuked Black Arts Movement as the prototypically essentialist aesthetic in an effort to make her case against being critically "prescriptive"; once again, the more recent example of Walker's womanism is conspicuously absent.[28]

Between the celebratory notes of pro-womanist advocates and the discourse of silence produced by major black feminist critics, then, there is room for a judicious critique capable of evoking at once the formidable and fragile character of womanist theory. Walker's womanism compels analysis if the full import of its cryptic content is to be realized. This content, as I indicated earlier, embodies simultaneously a critique of white (Euro-American) feminist sensibilities and the privileging of an oppositional (black and Third World) womanist consciousness. My objective in this book is to bring the discussion of womanism to a threshold of comparative textual analysis to allow for an expansive view that both supports and challenges the values and assumptions underlying Walker's disagreement with white feminist praxis.

Each of Walker's three core womanist claims—audaciousness, woman- and community-centeredness—finds support in the exigencies of life lived outside the privileged aegis of whiteness and maleness. The first of these—rebellious, audacious behavior—is a rich, self-affirming psychological resource that facilitates survival advantage in the social pecking order. African American women's culture, to cite the example most familiar to Walker, is a highly developed resistance zone infused with womanist directives. Pivotal among these is "womanish" behavior, a gesture of defiance with which the black woman-child responds to the unequal distribution of power in society. As a means of overstepping boundaries in familiar, often familial, settings, womanist audacity becomes in the wider social context an unbidden demolisher of arrogant authority. Paule Marshall's girl-heroine, Selina Boyce, in *Brown Girl, Brownstones,* Toni Morrison's rebel-heroine, Sula, and the consummate heroine, Sojourner Truth, for example, capture this unmistakable quality that runs through black womanhood.[29] Its evocation by Walker within feminism serves to distinguish black feminists' many-sided offensive against patriarchal proscription from their white counterparts' single-minded focus on gender inequality. For Walker, the white feminist bulwark against sexual oppression falls short of the intrepidity that compels the womanist to turn over every stone in the complicated masonry of power relations.

Woman-centeredness, the second key womanist principle, seems at first not only to contravene the unity-seeking ideological position embodied in the third core element of womanism but also to overlook the pro-woman imperatives that constitute white women's prolonged history of sexual politics. It is more likely, however, that Walker brackets a woman-centered unconscious in an effort to direct attention to the construction of black womanhood, a process that configures black female identity as a site of both self-empowerment and affiliation. "Only the BLACK WOMAN can say 'when and where I enter, in the quiet, undisputed dignity of any womanhood . . . then and there the whole *Negro race enters with me,*'" Anna Julia Cooper agonistically declares in *A Voice from the South.*[30] The idea is reiterated in *Tomorrow's Tomorrow,* even though Joyce Ladner downplays the indomitable image of the black woman: "In many ways the Black woman is the 'carrier of culture' because it has been she who epitomized what it meant to be Black, oppressed and yet given some small opportunity to negotiate the different demands which the society placed upon all Black people."[31] Both statements subsume the distinct cultural space inherent in black women's experience and the sensibilities forged therein. If womanists "prefer women's culture, women's emotional flexibility . . . and women's strength" (*Gardens,* xi), it is because female self-love, like Sojourner Truth's, or Selina's, or Sula's, is a bastion against the cruel fact of hegemonic dominance. Woman-centeredness mirrors to the womanist the fragmented world around her and the need to seek connection.

Thus, the third core womanist tenet posits what I call "whole(some)ness," a sense of emotional connection between self and Other that reverses the effects of long-term social divisions. The bonding impulse has historically been a powerful determinant in the health of the black body politic. From a painful history of physical and psychic disjuncture has emerged the phenomenon Michael Awkward describes as "Black culture's insistence on unity, even in the face of powerfully divisive opposition."[32] The ideology of black unity throws into necessary relief the incompatible psychic duality memorialized in W. E. B. DuBois's characterization of black identity: "One ever feels his two-ness—an American, a Negro; two souls, two thoughts; two unreconciled strivings, two warring ideals into one dark body, whose dogged strength alone keeps it from being torn asunder."[33] The countervailing pull toward whole(some)ness thus dramatizes the desire to heal a body politic riven by the corrosive forces of history.

Frantz Fanon, in his assessment of racially specific investments, traced the concept of "two-ness" to its colonial roots: "The colonial world is a Manichaen world. It is not enough for the settler to delimit physically . . . the place of the native. As if to show the totalitarian character of colonial exploitation the settler paints the native as a sort of quintessence of evil."[34] To return to "the sphere of psycho-affective equilibrium" involves, for Fanon, an "attach[ment] . . . to a cultural matrix" and, inevitably, the manifest desire for individual and collective wholeness.[35] The return, I believe, is also gendered, paving the way for male-driven nationalistic impulses and female expressions of a broader humanism.

The latter assertion is grounded in the historical facts of black and Third World women's protracted struggle against multiple forms of oppression and barriers to self-growth. "The hearts of Afro-American women," Fannie Barrier Williams declared, "are too warm and too large for race hatred. Long suffering has so chastened them that they are developing a special sense of sympathy for all who suffer and fail of justice."[36] Anna Julia Cooper, another speaker before the World's Congress of Representative Women in 1893, underscored the importance of Williams's statement by exhorting her white female audience to adopt a politics of inclusion: "The cause of freedom is not the cause of a race or a sect, a party or a class,—it is the cause of human kind, the very birthright of humanity." And, in an unmistakably critical tone, she warned that woman's cause is not won until her "wrongs are . . . indissolubly linked with all undefended woe."[37] Maria Stewart paved the way both literally and thematically for these nineteenth-century political and literary activists. Recognized as the first black female public speaker, Stewart issued a clarion call for racial unity in anticipation of a multiracial union between her people and the rest of humanity: "I am of a strong opinion, that the day on which we unite, heart and soul . . . that day the hissing and reproach among the nations of the earth against us will cease."[38]

More recently, Bessie Head, artist-guide of southern Africa, lent her deeply spiritual voice to the theme of a common humanity, Walker's third characteristic of womanism. Reflecting on the "attitudes of love and reverence to people" that govern her art, she admitted to appropriating "the word God . . . to deflect people's attention into offering to each other what they offer to an unseen Being in the sky. Where people are holy to each other, war will end, human suffering will end."[39] Visionary, brooding, and alone, Head took refuge in her secular religion of human love.

Clearly, Walker's womanist worldview has a strong grounding in historical and cultural facts which in turn have had a determining effect on black female subjectivity. Less clear, however, is whether womanism can absorb the shocks of an equally strong essentialist undertow. Walker's univocal black/ Third World female subject partakes in the same universalist logic that surfeited its white, Anglo-American counterpart, and if the analogy seems overdrawn, one need only recall the wave of anger over the exclusionary practices of white feminist theorists and critics that crested with the search for alternative visions of womanhood and female creativity. Happily, this search has led to the present state of competing feminisms, thwarting any effort to privilege a particular brand of femininity. Deracializing black feminist thought, however, has proved difficult, probably because pariah memory dies hard. In the peroration to her "talking" book, *The Coupling Convention,* Ann duCille speaks eloquently and unequivocally to the race question in African American literary practice:

> For all our rhetoric about race as socially constructed rather than biologically determined, much of our critical and cultural theory still treats race as natural and transhistorical. To a large extent contemporary tradition building and canon construction are rooted in reified notions of culture as based on race, encapsulated in race. Other imperatives of identity formation, including gender, often become excess baggage not only in the invention of an African American literary tradition but also in the development of a black feminist canon based on the belief in an essential, definitively black female experience and language.[40]

One of my objectives is to identify womanism as a major strand in this essentialist pattern of "identity formation." Walker's race-based womanist theory, I will argue, ignores the fluid and shifting nature of subjectivity, a fact conducive to crossings between such demarcated borders as black/white, male/female, womanism/feminism. Ironically, it is a fact with which Walker is all-too-familiar. In her foreword to Agnes Smedley's novel, *Daughter of Earth,* Walker concedes the fluidity of the female subject when she claims that Smedley, "poor, white, nearly slave-class in the 'free' 'democratic' United States where all *whites* at least are alleged to have an equal chance at 'making it'—connects herself . . . to all people of her class and vision, regardless of color or sex."[41]

And while Walker has never failed to demonstrate her racial and cultural difference from Virginia Woolf and Flannery

O'Connor (two white women writers she holds in high esteem), she is ever conscious of the ties that bind them.[42] Her avowed affinity to Woolf and O'Connor underscores the prescriptive nature of the womanist project. Indeed, it is no coincidence that until *The Color Purple*, as chapter 3 in this study will demonstrate, Walker herself is situated outside the womanist dispensation. Her coming-into-womanism testifies to the fact that black/Third World womanhood is complicated and various, neither the monolithic bogey of early Western feminist discourse nor the coherent subject of womanist construction.

Poststructuralist disdain for essentialism, however, should not blind us to the fact that womanist theory registers a critique of white feminist literary practice and offers a model of resistance against hegemonic domination. Walker's assertion that "womanist is to feminist as purple is to lavender" strikes a theme that disturbs conventional thinking about racial gender and therefore warrants as much scrutiny as her racially essentialist claim. Positing womanism as a problematic, therefore, I intend to simultaneously affirm and interrogate its premises via a close reading of selected texts by white and black feminist writers: *Mrs. Dalloway, The Middle Ground, The Color Purple,* and *The Joys of Motherhood,* respectively. Rather than representing a simple oppositional division between feminist and womanist praxis, these texts offer an opportunity to verify womanist claims and at the same time to reveal their excesses. The first two texts typify, in my view, the kind of bourgeois, liberal feminism which, given its "tendency to overemphasize the importance of individual freedom over that of the common good," not to mention its reification of masculinity, is clearly the target of womanist critique.[43] In Virginia Woolf's *Mrs. Dalloway* I identify a pattern of ambiguous iconoclasm that militates against womanist ideals. My reading of Woolf's sexual, racial, and class politics reveals an ensemble of attitudes symptomatic of the privileged position from which, as womanist critique suggests, the white liberal feminist launches her attack against patriarchy. I note here a complex interplay between Woolf's critique of British patriarchy and her own investment within the dominant ideological economy.

Walker's deep admiration of Woolf provides an incentive for determining whether Woolf was capable of realizing womanism's revolutionary potential. To this end I conduct a womanist reading of *Mrs. Dalloway* that reveals Woolf to be both animated and enervated by the exigencies of her birth, her culture, and her time, an attitude that yielded contradictory messages of resistance and acquiescence.

In chapter 2 the ground shifts from Woolf's modernist disease with the social system to Margaret Drabble's naturalistic portrayal of female victimization in *The Middle Ground.* I identify in this novel a bio-deterministic model of female identity that runs counter to womanism's emancipating ethos. One of the most prolific and successful writers in England today, Drabble bridges the ground between Woolf and Walker, sharing with the former a common cultural and feminist tradition (not to mention the great tradition according to F. R. Leavis) and with the latter the cultural and feminist ferment of these times.

Chapter 3 examines Walker's painful preparation in womanist philosophy, culminating in the epiphanic achievement of *The Color Purple.* The novel, I submit, is a true watershed of the author's (r)evolutionary womanist aesthetic. Its combative call for individual and collective freedom from the constraints of gender, race, class, sexuality, and nationality reverberates with the insistence of an old-time religion. The text's audacity fascinates as much as its message, calling into question, in dialogical fashion, the tame tactics of engagement deployed in the preceding texts. This chapter also delineates the cruel ordeal of Walker's womanist awakening, a cathartic experience replete with suggestion for (white) feminist re-vision. The last chapter considers *The Joys of Motherhood* by Buchi Emecheta, a novel that challenges the idea of an intrinsically black womanist identity. Emecheta fits well within the intertextual framework of my argument, given her links and disaffinities with the other authors of this study. Race and culture set her apart from Woolf and Drabble but for over thirty years now England has been home to her, too, a concrete indication of affinity with these writers.

Shared racial, gender, and feminist identities between Walker and Emecheta should make for, according to Walker's hypothesis, a shared womanist sensibility. My reading of Emecheta's novel in chapter 4 points up evidence to the contrary, thereby revealing the essentialist flaw in womanism's central premise. The race-restrictive womanist idea further founders on its own expectations with the revelation of resonant links between and among these writers.

An interpretive method, like mine, that holds white women writers to black/Third World women's standards points to an entirely new zone of critical discourse fraught with possibility for improved relations within feminism. If indeed difference has displaced sisterhood in the grammar of identity politics, then, as Minrose Gwin advises, "it seems important that we as black and white women together not only examine how we read and write biracial female experience, but that we understand how we are read as others in literature, in critical and theoretical conversation, and in life—by other women." Gwin rightly acknowledges that "black women have been doing [this] for centuries," while "white women are just beginning to learn how to do [so]."[44] Enter womanism, its chief virtue being its capacity to mirror to white feminist critics and writers images of the white female subject as Other. The big promise of womanism, therefore, is its function as a trope of otherness and my reading of difference through womanist eyes is, ultimately, the primary purpose of this book.

Finally, the term aesthetics, as deployed here, denotes the politics of representation rather than the linguistic experimentation generally associated with Stéphane Mallarmé, Oscar Wilde, or Virginia Woolf.[45]

1

Mrs. Dalloway

A STUDY OF WOOLF'S
SOCIAL AMBIVALENCE

It is not always the difference itself that feels most raw in feminist
encounters, it is the sense that some women have a continued self-
interest in refusing to acknowledge inherited inequalities that
others are not in a position to forget.

Mary Childers, *Conflicts in Feminism*

"I am not one and simple, but complex and many," Bernard
declares in *The Waves*, capturing a sense not only of the novel's crisis of identity but of Woolf's as well.[1] More than sixty
years later the attempt to understand and define Woolf's multiple personality has resulted in one of the most successful
critical enterprises in modern literary history. Among the
panoply of facts and interpretations of Woolf's life and art,
two contradictory impulses stand testimony to the daunting
complexity of her character; together they have fueled much
contemporary debate about her feminism. The first impulse
denominates Woolf as a founding feminist who used the "tools
and weapons at her disposal . . . to name the enemy, to expose the collaborators, to create new models of resistance to
oppression."[2] This view credits Woolf with an iconoclastic
desire for social change, rooted in a deeply personal sense of

patriarchal oppression. The second impulse evokes a different reality, one based on privilege, both literary and material.[3] Drawing from both perceptions, I will examine the relevance of Walker's womanist critique of white liberal feminism in terms of the textual signs of Woolf's social ambivalence in *Mrs. Dalloway.*

Life, as Virginia Woolf knew it, was at once ecstatic and painful. From her early years in the upper-middle-class confines of the Stephens' home at Hyde Park Gate to the intellectual magic kingdom of Bloomsbury, Woolf straddled the extreme emotions of joy and grief, excitement and anguish. Growing up as daughter of the eminent Victorian man of letters, Leslie Stephen, Virginia and a large network of siblings enjoyed a variety of material comforts provided by her "well-to-do" parents—sailing, vacations, travel, knowing and being known by the literary elite of the day.[4] But mingled with these delights were the painful facts of young Virginia's lack of formal education (because of her gender), the puritanical sternness of her father, and the sexual molestation she suffered at the hands of her half-brothers, George and Gerald Duckworth. With the death of her mother, Julia, in 1895, thirteen-year-old Virginia suffered her first mental breakdown. The death of her half-sister Stella (whose love for and marriage to Jack Hills had given Woolf "a standard of love") only three months after her wedding began to impress upon Woolf's young mind the incredible cruelty of life. This impression was to grow deeper with the deaths of her father (prompting her second mental breakdown) and her brother, Thoby, at the tender age of twenty-six.

Woolf knew early on in life that sorrow had staked a claim on her right beside the pleasures guaranteed her by pedigree and fame. And the intensity of these antithetical experiences would force her into a lifelong artistic commitment to explore the meaning of reality, to cut beneath its surface in search of "the spiritual continuum which lives beneath the appearance of change, separation and disorder that marks daily life."[5] However, Woolf's gift of an extraordinary sensitivity to the harshness of external reality and her desire to thwart or lessen its grip on the individual seemed to collide with the mentality of exclusiveness typical of "a small circle of highly cultured men and women"[6] of which she was a respected member. Intimately familiar with the debilitating power of suffering, Woolf was conflicted about the suffering of the Other. She could extend to working women, for example, "aesthetic sympathy, the sympathy of the eye and of the imagination," but not "of the heart and of the nerves" because ultimately "it is much better to be a lady," for ladies "desire things that are ends, not things that are means."[7]

Being a "lady," a term rife with notions of wealth, leisure, and snobbery, presented particular problems for Woolf. To a large extent, it accounts for the tension that characterizes her thinking and, inevitably, her writing about the mentality of the ruling class. That Woolf should find it necessary to ask herself the question "Am I a Snob?"[8] is indicative of the pull she felt between empathy with and emotional distance from persons on the fringes of power or society. If, for instance, she felt her own victimization as a female strongly enough to launch the type of protest that has rightly earned her the status of revered foremother of contemporary feminist critics, it is also clear that Woolf's prototypical woman was "the educated man's daughter,"[9] who may have been socially surpassed by her upper-class male kin but was undoubtedly the working woman's superior.

Similarly, her condemnation of the colonizing impulse and her heroic effort to link it inextricably with patriarchal ideology left unchanged her own view of the nonwhite races. The "negro," Indian, or South American were still in her mind symbols of otherness, occupying physical and mental regions which in E. M. Forster's words, "civilization had not yet blessed."[10] "It is one of the great advantages of being a woman," Woolf writes in *A Room of One's Own*, "that one can pass even a very fine negress without wishing to make an Englishwoman of her."[11] This appropriative gesture, apart from corroborating Walker's charges against contemporary white feminists, offers a glimpse of Woolf's unapologetic pride in her cultural inheritance, the underside of her radical politics. The high cultural ground she takes in this and other encounters with the racial Other supports Mark Hussey's assertion that "[t]he only radical politics for Woolf was sexual politics."[12]

In her first novel, *The Voyage Out*, Woolf evidences this view of otherness in her re-enactment of Joseph Conrad's *Heart of Darkness*, locating in South America (rather than in Africa) the jungle that strips away from English men and women the civilizing qualities of communication, personality, consciousness, memory, self-control and replaces them with untamed, illogical emotions and, eventually, death. Here, even God is "undoubtedly mad," for no "sane person could have conceived a wilderness like this, and peopled it with apes and alligators."[13] The "great green mass" of the forest differentiates most forcefully between "us" (the rational English people) and "them" (the "soft instinctive" natives), its darkness flashing warnings of reprisal to anyone who crosses the dividing line (337, 348). The heroine, Rachel Vinrace, caught between self-control and untrammeled instinct, surrenders, like Kurtz, to overwhelming impulses (although hers are sexual, not cannibalistic as Kurtz's are) and, inevitably, to death. Woolf's novel, to borrow from Abdul JanMohamed's description of colonialist discourse, "purports to represent specific encounters with . . . the racial Other [but] the subtext valorizes the superiority of European cultures."[14]

Woolf understood the unique role material conditions play in shaping human life and the creative imagination. Not only did a writer need material comforts (such as "a room of her own" and money for travel and leisure) in order to be intellectually productive, but her material condition also determined the vision of reality that she would create. Woolf's own created worlds are not very distant from the one she inhabited: white, upper-middle-class, patently intellectual. That her fictional vision hovers around the world she lived in and does not spread widely enough to incorporate other ways of life is, perhaps, understandable. What is not so clear is the fact that although Woolf had a profound knowledge of oppression—its sources, methods of operation, and destructiveness—and was deeply distressed by it, her fictional exploration of rule by domination is marked by a profound ambivalence that tends to contradict her genuine concern.

Some feminist critics find this quality problematic and others see it as a sign of her mastery of the modernist idiom. Prominent among the former is Elaine Showalter, who criticizes Woolf for her "denial of feeling" (85) and for practicing and promoting an aesthetics of sexual renunciation (in the name of transcendent art). Critical theorists, like Toril Moi, in a counter-critique of their own, point to Showalter's failure to recognize the complex network of statement and counter-statement, approbation and derision, support and subversion that constitutes Woolf's textual strategy. Toril Moi rejects Showalter's reading of Woolf as essentialist and reductive and posits instead a Kristevan analysis that accounts for the ways in which Woolf deconstructs "the opposition between masculinity and femininity and therefore necessarily challenges the very notion of identity."[15] She argues that because Woolf's modernist aesthetic practice insisted on the dislocation and subversion of the binary patriarchal opposition of the sexes rather than on its affirmation, critics, like Showalter, who look to her fiction for an unconditional approbation of femaleness will continue to be disappointed.

In *Virginia Woolf and the Problem of the Subject*, Makiko Minow-Pinkney echoes Moi's call for a reading of Woolf in terms of Julia Kristeva's psychoanalytic theory in order to fully understand the revolutionary nature of Woolf's poetics. According to Minow-Pinkney, Woolf's "insistence on abolishing the sociological realism of an Arnold Bennett, that fiction become poetry, no longer representing but rather presenting or constructing reality," led her to modernist experiments designed to disrupt existing literary structures, as well as social ideologies, especially that of gender.[16]

While Showalter presents Woolf as a writer who betrayed her sex in order to gain entry into the male-dominated profession of writing, Moi and Minow-Pinkney portray her as a female artist who adeptly merged the self in language, not to efface that self but to render it symbolic. Neither critical position, however, has given sufficient emphasis to Woolf's ambivalence about marginalization, one that points up the conflict between her social standing, on the one hand, and her victimization, on the other. In other words, unlike Showalter, who sees Woolf as sacrificing her feminism at the altar of male domination, or Moi and Minow-Pinkney, who praise her for putting the disruptive quality of modernist prose to use in her ongoing campaign against the prevailing order, I detect in Woolf's fiction a dialectic between condemnation and maintenance of the systems of domination and I link this habit of thought to what Woolf herself described as the "immense effect of environment and suggestion upon the mind."[17] Victimized by a system that at the same time bestowed on her the rights of privilege, Woolf felt most acutely the stresses of self-division, and her fiction bears the mark of the strain.

Mrs. Dalloway, the novel in which Woolf intended "to criticise the social system and to show it at work, at its most intense,"[18] illustrates Woolf's vacillation between disapproval of, and support for, the ruling class. By the time she wrote this novel, Woolf had launched a new fictional style to counter writers she considered fact-prone, such as Arnold Bennett and John Galsworthy. *Mrs. Dalloway,* Woolf's first full-blown experiment with the new form, is, as a result, a novel of reverberating ambiguity.

The novel registers a scathing attack on British patriarchy and imperialism, personified as the goddesses of Proportion and Conversion, whose mission is "to stamp indelibly in the sanctuaries of others the image"[19] of the (white, privileged male) self. William Bradshaw, high priest of the twin hegemonic powers, embodies the mindless terror of domination. Vulture-like, he preys on human vulnerability, transforming his patients into "cases" (151) of medical neglect, exploitation, and experimentation. The term "case" in nineteenth-century medical discourse, according to Elaine Showalter, carried connotations of colonization and conquest, a fact that helps to explain Bradshaw's construction of his patients as irremediably Other.[20]

The colonization metaphor certainly speaks to his relations with the shell-shocked war veteran, Septimus Warren Smith, whose mysticism he sees as a threat to his own mystique of authority. Bradshaw's prescription for this uncontainable figure is "rest in solitude; silence and rest; rest without friends" (150), in short, "the death of the soul" (88). Like the native or female Other, Septimus is silenced and contained for case study. For her part, Mrs. Bradshaw, exemplifies the success of her husband's colonizing program. Beaten into "submission" and silence, her vitality drained, she maintains an appearance of well-being by "minister[ing] to the craving which lit her husband's eye so oilily for dominion, for power" (152). So neat is her transformation from a spirited woman to a model wife that only "a nervous twitch" here and a "fumble stumble" there remain to give away her "confusion" (152).

Buttressed by state approval and support, Conversion has spread through "the heat and sands of India, the mud and swamp of Africa . . . dashing down shrines, smashing dolls and setting in their place her own stern countenance" (151). Woolf was acutely aware of the fact that England's expansionist fervor did more than simply plunder foreign lands; that it also stripped the conquered of self-identity, replacing it with a European construct of otherness. In her essay "The Novels of E. M. Forster," Woolf is pleased with what she considers Forster's deviation from the standard depiction of colonized people. She writes: "The people too, particularly the Indians, have something of the same casual, inevitable quality. They are not as important as the land, but they are alive. No longer do we feel in England, that they will be allowed to go only so far and no further lest they may upset some theory of the author's."[21] The statement provides a valuable clue concerning Woolf's empathy for the colonized subject and her own difficulty with the representation of difference.

The critique of imperialism and patriarchy in *Mrs. Dallo-*

way (Conversion and Proportion) betrays Woolf's strong anti-militaristic prejudice. In the text Septimus, like Shadrack in Toni Morrison's *Sula*, symbolizes the inexorable convergence of war and self-destructive passions. This insight is lost, however, on the custodians of culture, like Peter Walsh who, newly arrived from an outpost of Empire, takes a moment to express his admiration and respect for England's military men, the "Boys in uniform, carrying guns" whom "the will to conquer" had robotized. Woolf shares neither Walsh's delight at the sight of soldiers nor his respect for their heroism. Elsewhere she writes that the soldier in his splendid garb is not "a pleasing or an impressive spectacle. He is on the contrary a ridiculous, a barbarous, a displeasing spectacle" whose victories leave behind a trail of "dead bodies and ruined houses."[22] The connection between Bradshaw's tyranny over Septimus and Lady Bradshaw at home and Walsh's exploits in India is clear. Both actions have as a common goal the maintenance of domination. Lady Bradshaw's furs, the comfortable "home" where Septimus is to rest, and Peter's gift of a plough—these are all symbols of the elaborate camouflage system patriarchal imperialism has devised to disguise its sinister intent.

The condemnation of England's patriarchal imperialism in *Mrs. Dalloway*, however, is made to compete with a negative view of non-western cultures on the one hand and a sense of English cultural superiority on the other. In the novel, India connotes backwardness and failure. Peter Walsh's low standing among the upper class is emblematic of the disregard with which English society views India. An Oxford graduate who goes to India as a colonial officer, Peter is thought of by his old acquaintances as a failure. Clarissa set the devaluation of Peter in motion earlier when she dumped him for Richard Dalloway. Richard, "a man who cared only for dogs" (288) and who was clearly Clarissa's intellectual inferior, was going to be a parliamentarian, whereas Peter, whom she loved, seemed to be interested only in ideas: "the state of the world" (9). Years later, remembering that Peter "had married a woman [he] met on the boat going to India!" Clarissa can no longer hold back her contempt for those "silly, pretty, flimsy nincompoops" (10): young English women going to India to catch husbands, memsahibs-to-be.

Clarissa's opinion of Daisy seems to be influenced by what Jenny Sharpe describes as "[t]he stereotype of the memsahib . . . as a scapegoat of imperialism, the remedy and poison that both ensures racial segregation and threatens to undermine race relations,"[23] a further indication of politics of negotiation with which Woolf wrestles in this text. A scapegoat for Woolf's own sense of national guilt, Daisy is reduced to a bloodless caricature. Peter's own estimate of Anglo-Indian women may not be as reactionary as Clarissa's (or Woolf's) but it is certainly not high. There is no doubt in his mind, for instance, that Daisy, the woman he claims to have fallen in love with in India, "would look ordinary beside Clarissa" (64). He is still bitter over the fact that by rejecting him, Clarissa "had spoilt his life" (292), while Daisy, that "very charming, very dark . . . pretty girl . . . would give him everything" (238). Yet, as Susan Squier rightly points out, Peter "already seems to be tiring" of Daisy, while the flame he has carried in his heart for Clarissa for over thirty years still burns.[24] One of the reasons Peter has returned to England is to help secure a divorce for Daisy so that she can be free for a more stable relationship with him. Ironically, it is Clarissa who dominates his thoughts; Daisy appears only to provide temporary relief from an obsessive longing for an unattainable ideal. Indeed, as the text suggests, Daisy may very well have taken advantage of Peter's vulnerability, in which case she will deserve the rejection that awaits her:

> For it was very charming and quite ridiculous how easily some girl with a grain of sense could twist him round her finger. But at her own risk. That is to say, though he might be ever so easy, and indeed with his gaiety and good breeding fascinating to be with, it was only up to a point. (P. 237)

Daisy's "very dark" skin is a significant detail in her unflattering portrait. Juxtaposed with Clarissa's "very white" skin, it conjures up the conventional dark-light metaphoric equation which locates both women on different sites in the value con-

tinuum. Sally Seton, whose "extra-ordinary beauty," "aban-
donment," "dark" skin, and daring are attributed to "the
French blood in her veins" (48), stands above Daisy. The ten-
derness Woolf shows here for the French woman may stem
from her own ancestral ties with France (Julia Stephen's
mother was half-French). Her feelings about India, where her
mother was born, on the other hand, reveal her deep anxieties
over racial and cultural difference.

Signifiers of Orientalism in the text are numerous.[25] Peter
Walsh, for example, a *persona non grata* at home in England
where everyone agrees with Lady Burton that he "should
have made a name for himself but hadn't" (273) and with
Clarissa that he is "a failure" (11), metamorphoses in the racial wilderness of India into a resourceful colonizer with "a
turn for mechanics" that richly rewards "his district" with "a
plough" (73). His sense of cultural superiority also underlies
his reputation as "the best judge of cooking in India" (237).
Newly returned "from the East" where "baboons chatter and
coolies beat their wives" (263), Peter is heartened by "the effi-
ciency, the organization" of "civilization" (229). His walk
along London's famous streets is actually an exercise in the
appreciation of "civilized" culture, an experience that is
heightened by his intimate knowledge of savage India.

Female-constructed "allegories of Empire," to borrow
Jenny Sharpe's apt phrase, betray nostalgic underpinnings
but they are no less racially determined. Lady Bruton, the
"grande dame" of Empire, brings up in the recollections of
her own adventures in India "some . . . uncommonly fine
[Indian] fellows" (274), a rare breed, no doubt, like the "fine
negress" of *A Room of One's Own*. For Miss Helena Parry, that
eighty-year-old "indomitable English woman," the East will
never shed its travel-book image: "For at the mention of India, or even Ceylon, her eyes slowly deepened, became blue,
beheld, not human beings . . . it was orchids she saw, and
mountain passes and herself carried on the backs of coolies in
the 'sixties over solitary peaks; or descending to uproot orchids . . . which she painted in water-colour (271).

In her reading of this scene, Jenny Sharpe warns against allowing "Helena's good eye" to veil the fact that "both art and English women . . . participate in the business of colonialism," by ensuring, for example, "the native's invisibility."[26] While Helena's gaze erases the natives, it also captures in silhouette a stereotype of the native as beast of burden. The image of the colonial woman being carried on the backs and shoulders of native men through the danger-infested backwaters of Africa and India is at the heart of the Western production of the racial Other.

Woolf cannot be compared to E. M. Forster's "middle-class gentleman" who "is engaged in admiring himself and ignoring the rest of mankind."[27] In *Mrs. Dalloway*, as in Woolf's other works, humanity is important and therefore the forces that threaten to destroy it (war, patriarchy, imperialism) are seen as enemies of the people, for Woolf truly believed that "we are a doomed race, chained to a sinking ship" and we must "mitigate the sufferings of our fellow-prisoners . . . decorate the dungeon with flowers and air-cushions" (117). Yet behind the metaphors lies a differentiated humanity: West and East, civilized and primitive, developed and fallow. And though Woolf viewed England with a critical, sometimes merciless eye, it remained for her (as much as for Lady Bruton) "this dear, dear land" (274). *Mrs. Dalloway* is filled with the sights and sounds of London that are, in effect, Woolf's own "moments of pride in England" (82). Glad that he has left behind India's "plains, mountains; epidemics of cholera" (72), Peter Walsh bristles with pride as he walks through Regent's Park:

> Admirable butlers, tawny chow dogs, halls laid in black and white lozenges with white blinds blowing, Peter saw through the opened door and approved of. A splendid achievement in its own way, after all, London; the civilization. (P. 82)

While the passage is part of the overall satiric portrait of Peter that focuses attention on his masculine culture complex, the paean to London contains elements of Woolf's own affection for the city. In a diary entry of February 1924, she wrote: "London is enchanting. I step out upon a tawny coloured magic carpet, it seems, and get carried into beauty without raising a finger" (61). The threat of World War I drew from Woolf a deep current of affection for London: "Odd how often I think with what is love I suppose of the City: of the walk to the Tower: that is my England: I mean if a bomb destroyed one of these little alleys with the brass bound curtains and the river smell and the old woman reading, I should feel—well, what the patriots feel" (313). The statement takes on disturbing resonance with the knowledge of Woolf's longstanding and, often virulent critique of the patriotic impulse, evident here in her characterization of Lady Bruton and unrelievedly heavy in *Three Guineas.*

Clarissa, like her creator, finds London irresistible and its "divine vitality" intoxicating. Drawn toward the city's incredible mix of sights and sounds, she equates London with life and the liberating spirit:

> In people's eyes, in the swing, tramp, and trudge; in the bellow and the uproar; the carriages, motor cars, omnibuses, vans, sandwich men shuffling and swinging; brass bands; barrel organs; in the triumph and the jingle and the strange high singing of some aeroplane overhead was what she loved; life; London; this moment of June. (P. 5)

Some of the finest poetic passages in the text are devoted to capturing London's beauty. In one such passage evening is evoked in terms that suggest female sexual desire and echo Clarissa's experience of *jouissance* in the streets of London:

> Like a woman who had slipped off her print dress and white apron to array herself in blue and pearls, the day changed, put off stuff, took gauze, changed to evening, and with the same sigh of exhilaration that a woman breathes, tumbling petticoats on the floor, it too shed dust, heat, colour; the traffic thinned; motor cars, tinkling, darting, succeeded the lumber of vans; and here and there among the thick foliage of the squares an intense light hung. (P. 245)

Writing *The Middle Ground* nearly forty years after Woolf's death, Drabble replaces her predecessor's rhapsodic rendering of London with a stark view that fits the spirit of her own age: "London, how could one ever be tired of it? How could one stumble dully through its streets, or waste time sitting in a heap staring at a wall? When there it lay, its old intensity restored, shining with invitation, all its shabby grime lost in perspective."[28] Drabble's metaphors and prosaic rhythms parody not only Woolf's lyrics but her magical city as well. Woolf's "intense light" becomes an "old intensity," shining not on "the thick foliage of the squares" but rather on "shabby grime" and human dung-heaps. Postcolonial exigencies, what Louise Bennett calls "colonization in reverse,"[29] have transformed London from the site of private acts mapped in Woolf's writings into a theater of social discontent. The assorted implications, discussed in chapter 2, help to explain the aesthetic tension between Drabble and Woolf.

Mrs. Dalloway also illustrates Woolf's ambivalence about class difference. While the text exposes the sterility, parochialism, and self-indulgence of the upper class, the subordinate class, represented by Doris Kilman and Septimus Warren Smith, is neither held in high esteem nor offered as a healthy, viable alternative to the dominant order. Rather, Woolf's choice of an individual who embodies the potential for change and spiritual growth is Clarissa Dalloway, the incurable society woman who, nonetheless, has managed to retain the liberating qualities of self-criticism and love of life.

Woolf's salvos fired at individual members of Clarissa's class do serious damage to the group as a whole. Hugh Whitbread, for example, symbolizes upper-class effeteness at its worst. Obsequious, vain and greedy, Hugh is "a perfect specimen of the public school type" (110) whom Forster described as having "well-developed bodies, developed minds, and undeveloped hearts."[30] Hugh has made a career out of ingratiation: "For he likes nothing better than doing kindnesses, making the hearts of old ladies palpitate with the joy of being thought of in their old age, their affliction" (263). The sad truth, however, is that Hugh does not command the respect of those he tries so hard to please. Lady Bruton may need his writing skills, but she likes Richard Dalloway better. Richard, himself only a slightly improved version of the public school type, drops his guard for a moment to express his disgust at the way Hugh treats a sales clerk in a jewelry store on Conduit Street where he has entered to buy his wife a Spanish necklace. Refusing to do business with an inferior, Hugh pompously dismisses the clerk as "a mere boy," prompting Richard to walk away from such "an intolerable ass" (173). Sally Seton, from whom Hugh once tried to steal a kiss, thinks he is utterly contemptible: "He's read nothing, thought nothing, felt nothing" (110). Peter Walsh's damning summation of Hugh's character points up the seriousness with which Woolf viewed this class's violation of human decency: "Villains there must be, and God knows the rascals who get hanged for battering the brains of a girl out in a train do less harm on the whole than Hugh Whitbread and his kindness" (263).

The members of this decadent class have a matriarch in Lady Bruton. A relic from the nineteenth century, Millicent Bruton is "a strong martial woman, well nourished, well descended, of direct impulses . . . and little introspective power" (164). Her influence, money, and governing-class lineage, however, can do nothing to alleviate the heaviness of body and spirit that plagues her in old age. Hers is a life frozen in England's imperial past. Not to feel altogether empty, she whiles away her time on a project emigrating young, promising men and women "born of respectable parents and setting them up in Canada with a fair prospect of doing well in Canada" (164). But like Hugh's favors and Lady Bradshaw's child welfare and epilepsy campaigns, Lady Bruton's emigration project is a sham, a cover for her "pent egotism" (164). Woolf's depiction of Lady Bruton as the consummate patriot is as devastating as it is comic: "And if ever a woman could have worn the helmet and shot the arrow, could have led troops to attack, ruled with indomitable justice barbarian hordes and lain under a shield noiseless in a church . . . that woman was Millicent Bruton" (274–75).

The rapid-fire weapon Woolf deploys here is, of course, satire and it cuts through Lady Bruton's fanatical patriotic fervor ("being a soldier's daughter" (274)) to implicate English women in British imperialism. For while these women were excluded from the militaristic project of colonial domination, they lent support to it in a variety of ways, including fanatical patriotism such as Lady Bruton's.[31]

Millicent Bruton's characterization contains a feature shared by other members of her class and despised by Woolf, namely, intellectual poverty. Nearly every member of this self-indulgent social stratum is intellectually deficient. Lady Bruton, it is ironically suggested, did not acquire her patriotic zeal from reading Shakespeare; Clarissa, her love of Shakespeare notwithstanding, muddles Armenians and Albanians; Richard dismisses Shakespeare outright; Hugh, as Sally Seton points out, has never read anything; Dr. Bradshaw simply cannot fit reading into his busy schedule; and Lord Gayton and Nancy Blow, guests at Clarissa's party, are brainless beauties who simply "looked; that was all. That was enough" (269). The indictment is severe and hints at Woolf's own formidable literary qualities. Clarissa is spared the brunt of this attack, her fondness for Shakespeare made to mirror her creator's.

Clarissa's parties, however, celebrate the privileged mediocrity of the upper class and, therefore, they do not escape Woolf's satiric eye. In the first place, they set the sumptuous idleness of the monied class in bold relief against the dull, work-filled existence of their servants. The novel opens with the day of one such party. Clarissa decides to shop for the flowers herself because she wants to take "a plunge" into the fresh morning air. Meanwhile, Lucy, her maid, is engaged in draconian tasks, including unhinging the doors in order to clean them. Later, after ambling on Bond Street, Clarissa returns home where her servants have not had a moment's rest from work. That evening, the prime minister's grand entry at this gathering of self-important people frittering away their time in idle, meaningless chitchat is juxtaposed with a scene from the kitchen where Mrs. Walter, the head cook, is knee-deep in drudgery "among the plates, saucepans, colanders, frying pans, chicken in aspic, ice-cream freezers, pared crusts of bread, lemons, soup tureens, and pudding basins which, however hard they washed up in the scullery seemed to be all on top of her on the kitchen table, on chairs" (251). The servant class in the novel is, like the Indian Other, an invisible presence, relegated to silence and servitude. Lucy, the only member of her class to be given a voice, parrots the message Richard had left with her for Clarissa: "Mr. Dalloway, ma'am, told me to tell you he would be lunching out" (43). Throughout the text, Lucy is spoken to by Clarissa, spoken for by the narrator, and fitted with work-restrictive thoughts, a servile manner, and selflessness.[32]

Clarissa's party both enacts the class gap at home and provides a friendly forum for anecdotal impressions about strategies of containment. Peter Walsh attends, among other reasons, to find out from the parliamentarian, Richard Dalloway, what the British government's plans are for India, a weighty concern given his professional and personal investment in this colonial outpost. Bradshaw also has an informational item. He mentions the result of a "case" he has been working on: the young man "had killed himself" by jumping out a window (279). With the exception of Clarissa, whom the news jolts into a momentary sense of vulnerability, this group of emotionally inert persons responds to the tragedy only from the standpoint of stiff laws that will curb such impulse. "In this way," one critic of Woolf's novel notes, "the living Septimus becomes a category, his life an 'it' to be considered by government committees drafting legislation."[33]

But just as an undertow of racial bias cuts through Woolf's anti-imperialistic stance in *Mrs. Dalloway,* so is her opposition to the spirit of the governing class undermined by a negative view of the working class. Doris Kilman and Septimus Warren Smith are certainly victims of a lazy, dehumanizing bourgeoisie but Woolf does not see them as fitting substitutes for the ruling class. Doris Kilman is the quintessential victim turned malcontent. She feels cheated by the world, which has denied her the pleasures of charm, beauty, money, freedom of association, and has bestowed these precious commodities on Clarissa Dalloway instead. Her hatred of this usurper is so intense as to require a religious purging. Having lost her teaching job during the war for being sympathetic towards the Germans, Kilman now views Clarissa's pampered life with consuming envy. Her revenge is as deadly as her hate. Not only does she try to steal Elizabeth away from her mother, but she also assumes, an attitude of moral superiority, with suffering as the qualifying credential. Her total lack of inner life leads Rachel Bowlby to conclude that she is "a nineteenth century specimen rudely repackaged and sent on, complete with religious faith whose anachronism in the secular Dalloway society is underlined by its fundamentalist excess."[34] I would argue, however, that Woolf's demonization of Kilman has more to do with her class than her outmoded religiosity. Woolf herself admitted in her letter to Margaret Llewellyn Davies that the gap separating working class women from those of her own class was "impassable" and that transgressing the barriers "so that life will be richer and books more complex" was possible "but only when we are dead." The pronoun "we" denotes Woolf's sisterhood of privilege from which the working class women about whom she writes in this letter are excluded. But while Woolf could at least conceive of extending "aesthetic sympathy" to these women, she feels hardly any for Doris Kilman.[35] Instead Kilman's messianic sense of victimization is made to seem as oppressive as Bradshaw's medical methods. Both aim to subdue and convert.

The second exemplar of Woolf's negative view of the working class is Septimus, whose spiritual kinship with Clarissa and his victimization at the hands of Bradshaw and Holmes combine to create an impression of him that is initially sympathetic. It seems, however, that Septimus is as much a symptom of his society as he is a victim. Moreover, he shares this characteristic with Clarissa, the society woman who pays for her "sin" of capitulation with a tinge of social conscience. However, because Woolf identifies with the upper-class Clarissa and not with her working-class counterpart, Clarissa's self-contradiction is handled in a gentle and more sympathetic fashion. Like Clarissa, Septimus once sought social rank. Just as Clarissa had sacrificed love for material comfort, Septimus gambled the security of home life and an incipient literary career for the chance of becoming an overnight success story in London. Yet it is Septimus who is the butt of the narrator's scorn because "a clerk," a "half-educated" one at that, aspires to follow the path of "great men" about whom "the world has read later when the story of their struggles had become famous" (126–27). The upstart in him turns to World War I when London fails to reward quickly. Confronted with the horror of war—and, by extension, the reality of his choices —Septimus looks for another quick fix. He snatches Rezia from her creative, life-affirming environment in Italy only to drag her through the muddy waters of the death of the soul.

Close reading of the novel reveals that Woolf does a conceptual turnaround with Septimus's character. Having endowed him with surface qualities befitting Clarissa's male counterpart (both are social aspirants as well as misfits, both marry not for love, enjoy Shakespeare and poetry), Woolf abandons him at the deeper level of psychological reality in favor of Clarissa, the highbrow with the penchant for life. In typical highbrow fashion Clarissa desires "things that are ends, not things that are means" and it is the pure, unadulterated state of being, the life principle itself, that interests her. She is aware, like Septimus, of life's snares but, instead of allowing them to entangle her, she brushes them aside and continues her "upright" stride towards self-realization. Kilman and Bradshaw, for instance, make life intolerable for those they see as flawed or weak but, Clarissa intuitively asks, who is to say "of anyone . . . that they were this or were that?" Indeed her belief system values enemies as much as friends. And so during those moments of taking stock, when Clarissa confronts the enemy within (her snobbery, materialism, conventionality), she is not defeated. Self-reproach yields to celebration, to the wish for little kindnesses and, above all, the desire to bring people together. Custom has taught her that even "the Gods, who never lost a chance of hurting, thwarting and spoiling human lives were seriously put off if . . . you behaved like a lady" (117). Believing herself to be both separate and connected, Clarissa sees life and death as manageable experiences. Alive, she has chosen to be doggedly individualistic but, in death, there is a chance for atonement when, transcendentally, her "unseen" part survives in the "people" and "places" that she is convinced, "complete her" (231). Septimus lacks this sense of connection and is therefore vulnerable to destruction.

Feminist criticism got its first wind by simultaneously valorizing and condemning Virginia Woolf and two decades later the contradiction remains unresolved. The bone of contention is the degree of Woolf's commitment to feminism. Advocates agree with Jane Marcus that Woolf is the undisputed foremother of feminist criticism, the inventor and initial investigator of the term "patriarchy" and clearly the model for contemporary feminists in the effort to refurbish women's literary image.[36] These critics point to *A Room of One's Own*, *Three Guineas*, and countless essays and letters as incontrovertible evidence of Woolf's woman-centeredness. In her fiction, they agree, propaganda takes a back seat to art, yet even there Woolf's feminism still exists, in subversive but no less forceful fashion. Makiko Minow-Pinkney, using poststructural linguistics, analyzes Woolf's skillful management of the semiotic and symbolic spheres of language to undermine patriarchal hegemony.

According to Margaret Homans in *Bearing the Word: Language and Female Experience in Nineteenth-Century Women's Writing*, this same covert activity results in the reconstitution, the re-representation of the myth of female subordination. Homans and Minow-Pinkney are actually restating in the language of contemporary literary theory and psychoanalysis a point made earlier in "Emphasis Added: Plots and Plausibilities in Women's Fiction" by Nancy K. Miller, who contended that embedded in the female plot is a subtext of revolt against "the constraints the [male] maxim places on rendering a female life in fiction.''[37] Woolf critics are therefore constantly scratching the surface of her fiction to reveal another Woolfian subversive subtext.

Less loyal Woolf critics find a subtext of their own but, as Elaine Showalter's analysis of *A Room of One's Own* shows, it is one of acquiescence rather than resistance. Showalter argues that Woolf's promotion of androgyny as the appropriate outlook for the woman writer was an act of acquiescence of the male literary establishment of her day, a way to ensure that she remained "impersonal and inconspicuous" and, therefore, admissible (281). There is no doubt that literary tradition held special importance for Woolf. She was most certainly concerned about its "continuity," as Showalter avers (280), but, judging from Woolf's denunciation of the realists, Bennett and Galsworthy, she was also eager to give the tradition a modernist stamp. This meant that what was once coherent, unequivocal, and whole would now be, in Woolf's own words, "spasmodic," "obscure," "fragmentary,"[38] a philosophical and stylistic attitude that allowed for what Marianne DeKoven aptly describes as "modernism's simultaneous assertion and denial of rebellious impulses."[39]

A comparison of two short stories, "A Society," taken from a period (1917–22) predating Woolf's modernist consciousness, and "A Woman's College from Outside," written around 1925 (the year *Mrs. Dalloway*, Woolf's modernist experiment, was published), shows that Woolf's feminist ambiguity is tied to her involvement in modernism. "A Society" is the type of fiction Woolf later decries in *A Room of One's Own*. The author of "A Society" is clearly "attend[ing] to a personal grievance" (76), the same breach of literary faith she would accuse Charlotte Brontë of committing in *Jane Eyre* (24). And, interestingly enough, her complaint is no different from Charlotte Brontë's: the sex-based value system that devalues women and overvalues men.

"A Society" is the story of a small group of women who form "a society for asking questions" that should lead to an answer to the bigger question of why women continue to give birth to men who destroy the world. The women conduct their investigations in the male bastions of academia, the law, and the military (Woolf's favorite targets) and as each narrates her encounter with what they discover is an implacable patriarchy, it becomes clear that their initial inclination to fault women for an oppressive sexual ideology is a grievous misapprehension. Male vanity and self-aggrandizement are very much independent of women's role as progenitors. These qualities are the by-products of socialization, a phenomenon Woolf refers to here as the "intellect." Unlike Simone de Beauvoir, Woolf in this story absolves women of complicity in their own oppression. "A Society" affirms its author's belief that the masculine complex is a singularly male construction:

> What could be more charming than a boy before he has begun to cultivate his intellect? He is beautiful to look at; he gives himself no airs; he understands the meaning of art and literature instinctively; he goes about enjoying his life and making other people enjoy theirs. Then they teach him to cultivate his intellect. He becomes a barrister, a civil servant, a general, an author, a professor. Every day he goes to an office. Every year he produces a book. He maintains a whole family by the products of his brain—poor devil! Soon he cannot come into a room without making us [women] all feel uncomfortable. . . . (P. 129)

The seemingly beneficent "they" in the above passage is actually a self-important patriarchy whose primary function is socio-psychological conditioning. Woolf thus anticipated the findings of such contemporary feminist theorists as Dorothy Dinnerstein and Michelle Z. Rosaldo, who state that sexual asymmetry is a product of culture, not nature. This point is underscored in "A Society" by two seemingly unrelated events: first, one of the sorority members sworn to the oath of non-procreation until after it has been determined whether the human race is worth perpetuating becomes pregnant during the investigation, and second, war breaks out. The pregnancy symbolizes nature's randomness while the war represents culture's self-conscious character. Like the domination of one sex by the other, war is a learned response. Childbearing, on the other hand, is as "natural" as the seasons. Woolf's society of women comes to realize that their initial blurring of the nature/culture boundaries was as mistaken as their impulse to blame women for the larger society's predicament. The story ends with a classic Woolfian proposition: Intellectual empowerment of women is an effective deterrent to war. As for the future woman, "Once she knows how to read there's only one thing you can teach her to believe in—and that is herself" (130), rather than believing in man's supposedly superior intellect, which causes war.

"A Woman's College from Outside" seems to suggest from its title a similar hard-line view of patriarchy, especially in light of Woolf's fascination with periphery as it relates to patriarchally ordered society. While she hastened to acknowledge the limitations of life on the social fringes, Woolf was equally aware of its enabling potential. In *A Room of One's Own*, for instance, the narrator smarts from being barred from the library, a male bastion of power, but she is also cheered by the thought that "unpleasant [as] it is to be locked out . . . it is worse perhaps to be locked in" (24). Later in *Three Guineas* Woolf strongly urged the creation of an "Outsiders' Society" of women (of which "A Society" is a prototype) that would challenge patriarchal practices, chief among them, the imperialistic mentality. Women would curb the male instinct for war by redefining patriotism: "The outsider will say, 'in fact, as a woman, I have no country. As a woman I want no country. As a woman my country is the whole world'" (109). "A Woman's College from Outside" seems, at first glance, to extend female boundaries even further by incorporating the outlawed subject of lesbianism, but its tone is markedly different from the determined aggressiveness deployed in "A Society." Propaganda has yielded to symbolism; pent-up anger has dissipated, replaced by a self-conscious prudence. Love between two women can only be a possibility, an unreachable "new world . . . at the end of the tunnel" (141). The nearly explosive excitement Angela feels from being kissed by Alice is blocked by pain and guilt. Angela's "discovery" that another woman can provide her with such sexual stimulation is, anticipating Clarissa's, "a thing not to be touched, thought of, or spoken about, but left to glow" in "her breast" (141).

Woolf's muted feminism in "A Woman's College from Outside" corresponds with her growing interest in a new literature. Exasperated by Arnoldian realism (and its heavily sociological bent) and yet equally uninspired by Joyce's solipsistic brand of modernism, Woolf was anxious to explore literary techniques of her own. "A Woman's College from Outside," written between 1922 and 1925, signals the shift from the discursive to the poetically cryptic and its attendant subordination of material reality to psychological verity, a move that would establish Woolf's "avant-guarde identity."[40] In this "Chloe likes Olivia" story (that rare look at female relationships outside a male context that Woolf, in *A Room of One's Own*, hoped would become a staple in women's writings) stylistic concerns predominate over thematic ones and the societally indelicate subject is concealed in a forest of symbolism. While Woolf felt too strongly about women, particularly their gendered inheritance, to abandon them for the lure of modernism, her own androgyny-based prescription for great literature drew her away from the declamatory posture of "A Society" towards the repressed tone of "A Woman's College from Outside" and the blatant ambivalence of *Mrs. Dalloway*.

By naming the novel "Mrs. Dalloway" rather than, say, "Clarissa Dalloway" or "The Hours," its original title, Woolf was trying to make certain that her point about the effects on women of patriarchal socialization did not go unnoticed. Clarissa, as Mrs. Dalloway, embodies the female personality split engendered by the convention of marriage. While her former vivacious, reckless self is not completely sloughed off, it recedes into the background to make room for the society matron, "mistress of silver, of linen, of china," and hostess par excellence. Her choice of Richard over Peter, in the first place, is a matter of social status, not passion. Smarter than Richard, Clarissa has nonetheless been deprived of a formal education, an act calculated to ensure her dependence on a man of means. Life as a parliamentarian's wife, however, is riddled with conflict for Clarissa. Surrounded by a spiritually dead elite, she struggles to preserve her "indomitable vitality." Her parties do retrace momentarily that vitality, though ostensibly they are her way of thanking Richard for providing her with a carte blanche lifestyle. Yet for all their enabling capacity, Clarissa's parties are far from ennobling. They hold up for scrutiny the morally decadent world in which she is willingly entrapped. Like Lilie Briscoe in *To the Lighthouse*, Clarissa is a free spirit—artistic, intuitive, probing—but unlike her unmarried counterpart who, at the end of the novel, is able to break through the enigma of existence and in so doing unleash a burst of creative energy, Clarissa cannot soar too high. She is tied down to the marital task of maintaining her husband's self-image and, by extension, British patriarchy. In the end, rather than solving an enigma as Lilie Briscoe does, Clarissa instead becomes one: a "terror" and an "ecstasy."

Clarissa is not the only female in the novel whose inner life is impoverished by marriage. Lady Bradshaw's "nervous twitch" that makes itself visible on occasion beneath her splendid garments betrays a weariness of body and soul that stems from the knowledge that she is as much a victim of her husband's venality as are his mental patients. Giving up salmon-fishing for a husband with a "twelve-thousand-a-year" income is a trade-off a sensible woman in patriarchal society is expected to make unquestioningly, but the truth is that Lady Bradshaw has been short-changed by the deal. Like Clarissa, not only has she had to barter her soul for a few more pieces of silver but her eight-to-nine-course dinners (a smaller version of Clarissa's parties) for "the professional classes" validate the oppressive patriarchal state. Rezia's trade-off at the other end of the social scale is equally devastating. Her native Milan seems a lost paradise, its sheltered gaiety usurped by a brooding somberness. Unloved yet loving, she feels cheated but she suffers alone because Septimus, her husband, is as self-centered as he is demented. The emotional abuse perpe-

trated on her points up women's precarious position in patriarchy in which even a victimized male can still wield power
over a female.

Functioning as a counterweight to the feminist consciousness in *Mrs. Dalloway* is a culturally conditioned view of women
as dependent, exploitable, and self-hating. Easily manipulated
by men, the women in the novel reserve their hostility and
suspicion for other women from whom they are totally alienated. Clarissa and Lady Bruton, for instance, having both experienced a loss of innocence and both carrying the burden of
privilege, could effect "a singular bond" (161). Instead, they
are bound by mutual hostility. For Clarissa, Lady Bruton's
aging face mirrors "the dwindling of life" (44) and reflects the
terrible fate that she believes awaits her. Millicent Bruton, the
woman of whom Woolf says "year by year her share [of life]
was sliced" (44), conjures up in Clarissa's mind the image of
death, especially her own. If the "heavy and drowsy" Lady
Bruton leaves Clarissa feeling "shrivelled, aged, breastless"
(45), Doris Kilman feeds on her soul like a parasite. Poor and
deprived, Kilman embodies her class's resentment of the rich
and privileged. Of significance, however, is the fact that it is
Clarissa—not Richard or any male wielder of power—who is
the target of Kilman's hatred. Ugly, plain and unloved, Kilman sees in the pampered and attractive Clarissa everything
she has been denied. Her scheme to turn Elizabeth against her
mother is, on the one hand, an attempt to pull Clarissa into
her world of pain. On the other, it perpetuates the woman-
against-woman mentality of the novel, with Clarissa's denial
of her love for Sally Seton providing a startling example.

Woolf's ambivalence toward lesbianism seen earlier in "A
Woman's College from Outside" is replayed in the relationship between Clarissa and Sally Seton. Once again a kiss
from another woman proves to be a revelatory experience:
"The whole world might have turned upside down! The others disappeared; there she was alone with Sally" (52). But the
"illumination" is quickly dimmed as Clarissa shuts off her
desire for Sally to continue her pursuit of a proper husband.

In an insightful essay on female writers and the modernist

tradition, Marianne DeKoven locates the characteristic ambivalence of such writers as Woolf, Stein, Rhys and Hurston
(among others) in a pull between the modernist desire for the
"new" and a female fear of male retribution for expressing
that desire. These writers' "content would have been too
threatening at the time. . . . It would have had to be watered
down or altered in some way that would have left it with a
less powerful impact than in these narratives as they stand"
(36). Woolf's feminist ambivalence clearly reflects this reality
but her racial and class "doubleness" may have a different
origin, namely, the conflict between her humanistic values
and her position of privilege. While Woolf's sexual self-
concept stood in opposition to the hegemonic representation
of femaleness, her racial and class attitudes were more akin to,
than distinct from, those of the dominant culture. As *Mrs.
Dalloway* illustrates, Woolf may have carried the burden of sex,
but race and class were burdens for others to carry.

2

The Middle Ground

DETERMINISM IN
A CHANGING WORLD

This culture of manipulated passivity . . . has every stake in opposing women actively laying claim to our own lives.

Adrienne Rich, *On Lies, Secrets, and Silence*

Born to middle-class parents two years before Virginia Woolf's
death in 1941, Margaret Drabble stood to inherit the educa-
tional and career opportunities Woolf had staunchly advocated on behalf of women of her class in *A Room of One's Own*
and *Three Guineas*. Woolf would have been mightily pleased by
Drabble's uncomplicated entry into Cambridge, that implacable bastion of male dominance which less than three decades earlier, had suffered a momentary loss of nerve over
Mary Carmichael's trespassing within its hallowed grounds
(*Room* 6–8). Drabble's honors degree in literature made possible a more thorough (though no more intimate) acquain-
tance with the English (and European) literary tradition than
Woolf could have realized on her own in her father's famed
library. Drabble's deft handling of the pressures of marriage,
motherhood, and career is further proof that Woolf's prophecy

of unrestricted female accomplishment had come to pass. The daughters of educated English men were now not only themselves educated but were also competing with their educated brothers in the once male-specific professions.

Sexual parity thus achieved on these two important fronts in the gender struggle, one would expect the vexing issue of female secondariness that Woolf confronted in her essays and fiction (albeit less pointedly in the latter) to simmer down in Drabble's fiction. On the contrary, major victories notwithstanding, the sex war is far from over. The effects of gender socialization that led to an intense but private struggle for Mrs. Dalloway, Mrs. Ramsey, and Lily Briscoe have reached explosive dimensions in Clara Maugham, Rose Vassiliou, and Kate Armstrong and to this roily state of sexual politics Drabble adds a Hardyesque element of fate and chance to create a psychic landscape populated by self-doubting, emotionally crippled women. Drabble's educated, career-oriented heroines are a far cry from Woolf's restively married women but they are less content and much more neurotic. Drabble casts a critical eye on feminist progress, tempering the euphoria of success with hard-boiled cynicism. Interestingly, in what is obviously a critique of her predecessor's restrictive modernist aesthetic, Drabble has noted that Woolf "articulate[d] sound principles" in her prose "about caring for the helpless, and bettering the lot of every woman" yet "she couldn't do it in fiction."[1] However, under the relaxed rubric of realism and a far less rigid social climate, Drabble hardly escapes Woolf's quandary.

In *The Middle Ground*, the novel in Drabble's canon that enacts most tellingly the dilemma of contemporary feminism, the metaphysical struggle that plagued Woolf's female characters has been replaced by existential paralysis, induced as much by an inexorable link with the past as by a gnawing uncertainty about the future. Two statements capture the mood of the novel: first, the narrator's remark in the opening pages that Kate, who "has run through what she now recognizes were the expected phases of life . . . doesn't know what will happen next, nor how to make it happen" (13), and second, Hugo's lament "that modern consciousness is so burdened with its own past that it has worked itself into a state of paralysis" (185–86). Uncertainty and paralysis are symptoms of the sense of powerlessness that presides over Drabble's deterministic universe. Unlike Woolf, who, according to Gillian Geer, desired to stay outside "the masculine world of fixity and determination," Drabble grounds herself firmly in a materialist world where women are trapped in gender and the races in separate mental spheres.[2] *The Middle Ground*, I will argue, both enacts and attempts to undermine Drabble's brand of social determinism, but before I examine how this process unfolds in the novel, I will first show how Drabble's early fiction sets the tone of unmitigated sexual determinism.

Drabble launched her writing career as a "women's novelist,"[3] an accolade she regards as inhibiting rather than liberating even though she acknowledges its half-truth: "All my first books," she is quoted as saying, "were written very much from the woman's point of view and they were narrated through the vision of women."[4] The other side of this confession is the troubling fact that her women's self-vision is tainted by patriarchal depictions of femaleness and their attempts at redefinition are doomed. Simone de Beauvoir's analysis of how "one is not born, but rather becomes, a woman" in *The Second Sex* provided Drabble with a philosophical grounding for her early novels which depict women as trapped in the prison-house of their sex.[5] She refers to Beauvoir's book as "wonderful material . . . that nobody had used and I could use and nobody had ever used as I would use it."[6] Drabble is right about her unique application of de Beauvoir's hypothesis of female immanence versus male transcendence: her female characters still lack the power of self-constitution (which Beauvoir sees as a singularly male trait), in spite of a successful feminist movement. While there are ample traces of this mentality in the later novels, including *The Middle Ground*, it pervades the early fiction.

Drabble's first young heroine, Sarah Bennett in *A Summer*

Bird-Cage, is certain from the very outset that it will take more than her first class honors English degree for her to be someone of value in a male-ordered society; hence, when asked the most logical question confronting every graduate, namely, what she plans to be, her response is, "I will be what I become, I suppose."[7] The novel dramatizes the process by which Sarah, like her privileged peers ("middle-class girls with no sense of vocation" [33]), becomes a woman. Sarah has both looks and brains but it is the former that she values more. Indeed, to her these qualities cannot coexist in a woman and therefore she cannot imagine herself as a university don: "You can't be a sexy don. It's all right for men, being learned and attractive, but for a woman it's a mistake. It detracts from the essential seriousness of the business" (198). Woolf's "Angel in the House," it seems, is a clearer influence on Drabble than her theory of androgyny.[8]

But lest Sarah be deemed as worthless as her "lovely, shiny, useless new degree" (9), Drabble hastens to inform the reader that there is a man in her life. Francis, whom Sarah met in her last year at Oxford, is pursuing graduate studies at Harvard. Her observation of the marriages of others, including her sister's, should thus be viewed not as idle pastime but as necessary preparation for her own likely union with Francis. But this kind of assurance merely underscores Sarah's depleted self-image. The "primary focus" of *A Summer Bird-Cage*, Ellen Cronan Rose aptly notes, "is not the status within patriarchy of an educated young woman like Sarah, but her psychology." Having "internalized" the attitudes of sexual conditioning, Rose argues, Sarah remains trapped in adolescence even as she longs for adulthood.[9]

Drabble extends this theme in *The Garrick Year*, where Emma Evans tries to cope with her own sexual fate through camouflage. The theater, which sustains her actor-husband, David, at the same time that it has stifled her chances of a fulfilling career, provides her with the opportunity for role-playing. As a wife and mother, the twenty-six-year-old Emma deeply resents the limitations and assumed inferiority of these roles, so she casts them off for two unconventional, but in her mind, attention-getting parts: freak and mistress. Emma believes "we are what we seem to be";[10] if David can, as commentator Nora Forster Stovel sees it, "mask his wishy-washy nature" with "rugged pretensions,"[11] and if Wyndham Farrar (Emma's lover) can have "all the attributes of quality without quality itself" (220), then Emma sees no reason why she cannot pull a trick or two of her own.

But reality, according to Drabble, is stronger than illusion and, in Emma's case, it manifests itself in her sexual rigidity, which brings an end to her passionless romance with Wyndham and throws her husband into the welcome arms of gloss-queen Sophy Brent. These incidents, combined with the near-drowning of her daughter, Flora, awaken Emma to the serious threat her dissembling poses to her marital and maternal identity. With Drabble's blessing, she quickly recasts herself into the conventional (and, the reader infers, her "natural") role of custodian of the institution of family. The novel ends with a picture-perfect scene of pastoral serenity showing the reconciled Emma and David with the children enjoying nature's beauty. She has redeemed herself and saved her family and that is all that matters: "Had David and I been two entirely different people, we might well that afternoon have been entirely happy; and even being what we were, we did not do too badly" (223). Reflecting on the suicide of her friend Julian, the closet homosexual whose feeble resistance against society's rigidly construed sexuality mirrors her own, Emma tries to rationalize her behavior with these self-consoling words: "Indecision drowned him. I used to be like Julian myself, but now I have two children, and you will not find me at the bottom of any river. I have grown into the earth. I am terrestrial" (221). The "cast iron lady" (220) has metamorphosed into "an earth mother" ready to bury "the pathological aspects of her personality . . . rigidity, compulsiveness, neurosis, frigidity, masochism," as well as her early resistance to being corsetted.[12] Mirroring Clarissa's relationship with Septimus, Emma finds enough succor in the self-destruction of Julian to

resume her arid marriage. But unlike Clarissa, Emma is stripped of the illusion of autonomy and made to clutch her natural role as mother.

In *The Millstone* the metaphor of concealment encapsulates
the main character within the emergent ideology of single
parenthood, thereby doubling the burden of female identity.
A sense of inexorability frames Rosamund Stacey's self-narra-
tive, from her recognition at the beginning of the novel that
"a pattern forms before we are aware of it, and that what we
think we are becomes a rigid prison making us" to her accep-
tance in the end that "there is nothing I can do about my nature, is there?"[13] Between these bookends the Drabblean drama
of women's biological entrapment unfolds against a benign
backdrop of material and intellectual privilege. Infinitely
clever, Rosamund devises a system of psychological gender-
crossing to free her mind from her shackled body. As Susan
Spitzer points out, Rosamund "will 'think like a man' in her
academic pursuits, refrain from expressing deep emotion in
her adult relationships . . . [and] relegat[e] her 'female' demands to the unconscious realm."[14] Two of these demands—
sex and maternity—are handled with professional precision.
Rosamund guards her virginity until her mid-twenties and
when in a drunken stupor she finally gives in, it is to the
effeminate George Matthews, rather than the sexually potent
Joe Hurt or Roger Henderson. The same deliberation accom-
panies her experience with motherhood: an abnormally neat
pregnancy and childbirth, followed by a self-absorbed connection with Octavia, her baby-cum-trophy. Being a woman
in a man's world is indeed a weighty problem that neither the
given symbols of her class—money, education, industry—nor
the feminist principles her mother imbued in her can amelio-
rate. Rosamund's strategy of self-concealment may be the
cleverest ruse yet devised by a Drabblean heroine but it still
fails to hide her inability to grow.

The shift from the first-person narrative strategy of the first
three novels to the variety of storytelling techniques (intrusive
omniscience, third-person, interior monologue) in subsequent
works has been critically overstated as signaling Drabble's in-

tention to step out of the slough of sex into more airy regions of social transaction. The movement has been described as being "further away from the solipsistic spaces of the earliest novels" and as an artistic necessity to end the practice of "blindly inhabiting the district of her own experience."[15] There is no doubt that even before Drabble admitted to being "fed up" with women in a 1977 interview, she had purposefully begun to stretch her creative canvas beyond what she herself referred to as "the nose-in-the-washing-machine school of fiction" that characterizes her early works.[16] In *Jerusalem the Golden*, for example, Drabble tackles the standoff relationship between individual freedom and personal history, as she uproots Clara Maugham from the barren soil of her "soul-destroying grim industrial" hometown of Northam and transplants her into the golden worlds of Paris and London, where she blossoms outwardly but retains a crippled, loveless core.[17] In her biography of Arnold Bennett, Drabble acknowledges her "debt" to her distant relative and literary forefather for the environment-is-character idea that informs *Jerusalem the Golden*, although echoes of D. H. Lawrence are equally resonant.[18]

The Needle's Eye marks the turning point in Drabble's artistic consciousness even better than *Jerusalem the Golden* because not only does the author attempt for the first time to see the world from a man's point of view but she also enters that world of money, power, and law. Henceforth, as *The Realms of Gold, The Ice Age, The Middle Ground,* and *The Radiant Way* reveal, Drabble's canvas will be dotted with the ever-widening vistas of law, anthropology, geology, real estate, religion, and ecology.[19] Critics have generally viewed this move from nature to culture, from the personal to the universal, as heralding Drabble's maturity as an artist, a stance that lends credence to Sherry B. Ortner's argument that the conventional opposition between culture and nature, paralleling the split between male and female, is a patriarchal tool that devalues women.[20] Drabble, in effect, is being praised for moving from the petty subject of nature (women) to the weightier one of culture (men).

But as Drabble traverses the unfamiliar, male-identified

terrain of the later novels, she takes along her favorite theme of female identity, and her prognosis for a healthy, realizable female self is as dim as the portrait of womanhood that frames the first three novels. The fate of sex hangs over Drabble's women, sometimes sapping their physical vitality, at other times, their emotional or spiritual well-being and always their efforts at self-realization. *The Ice Age*, Drabble's vision of the wasteland that is contemporary Britain, ends with a chilling assessment of female possibility: "Alison there is no leaving. Alison can neither live nor die. Alison has Molly. Her life is beyond imagining. It will not be imagined. Britain will recover, but not Alison Murray" (295). In view of the destruction visited upon the land and its people by greedy, megalomanic men like Anthony Keating and Ken Wincobank, Drabble's denial of hope for Alison, one of the victims, on the grounds that she has a child with cerebral palsy strikes at the heart of feminist disapproval of Drabblean aesthetics. Elizabeth Fox-Genovese, reading Alison's fate as symptomatic of Drabble's anti-woman bias, notes with regret:

> Alison Murray's prison consists in her love for her cerebral palsy-inflicted child. The prisons that confine men . . . promise eventual release, sentences have a term, and confinement can serve to structure an internal freedom. . . . The prisons that ensnare women offer no such possibilities. Permanently bound to their own bodies, to their mothers and sisters, to their children, to their narcissism, women remain consigned to recurrence, reproduction, meaningless labor.[21]

Like the mothers before her—Emma Garrick, Rosamund Stacey, and Jane Gray (*The Waterfall*)—Alison Murray cannot transcend her biological self and integrate, as mother and actress, the mind-body split with which she is afflicted. For a woman in mid-life whose "beauty had for years been identity . . . , how could she ever make another, for the second half of her necessary life?" (94). Britain, on the other hand, also aging and, in addition, critically maimed, has a better chance of recovery. Its fate is in the hands of men like Anthony Keating, who, having played the money game and lost, can now turn to what Ellen Cronan Rose refers to as "the biggest game of all . . . 'the God Game.' "[22] If the implicit comparison of Anthony's change of heart to Paul's on-the-road-to-Damascus conversion is any indication, Drabble would rather bet on Anthony's new game than on Alison's sex-determined future.

If *The Ice Age* leaves Alison drained of hope and Britain "not in thrall, but a land passing through some strange metamorphosis . . . not defeated, but waiting still" (221), the succeeding novel, *The Middle Ground*, finds the nation in the throes of change and women in the depths of despair. *The Middle Ground* draws attention to the cultural mix of contemporary British society, the effects of urbanization and internationalization on life in London, and the status of a maturing feminist movement. The face of Drabble's England is ostensibly different from the one Woolf knew mainly because the once-colonizing nation has now been claimed by those it colonized. The guest lists of the parties that end both *Mrs. Dalloway* and *The Middle Ground* attest to the difference. Clarissa's company consists almost entirely of "the gentlemen [and ladies] of England" (*Dalloway* 25), the elite and governing class, including the prime minister himself. With the exception of the childless Peter Walsh and Clarissa's poor cousin, Ellie Henderson (who was given a last-minute invitation), each person in the group has, in Peter's words, "six sons of Eton" (289), a remark that is more significant for its gender and class implications than its accuracy.

Kate's guest list, on the other hand, is a mixed bag of race, class, sex, and nationality: the ordinary, marginal, and foreign who make the daily rounds in her crowded, "tiny house" (252). The Indians to whom Clarissa and her guests frequently refer in conversation are represented at her party by the Anglo-Indian, Peter Walsh, returning to London with the latest news from the Empire. Otherwise, they are relegated to the invisible realm of memory. In Drabble's novel such repression of the subjects of the Empire is no longer possible. Indeed, with the subsumption of the Empire into the postmod-

ern "global village," Drabble is inclined to invoke the sense
and sensibility embodied in E. M. Forster's advice to "connect" across "the rainbow bridge."[23] This desire, however,
collides with a deterministic vision that defies the womanist
concept of whole(some)ness. Drabble's self-description as
"egalitarian," that is, one who thinks "everyone should have
the same hand of cards when they're born," is, indeed, true to
womanist form.[24] Her added caveat—"I can't get over the fact
that they haven't"—constitutes what Walker would see as a
compelling reason for womanist intervention in feminism.

Drabble portrays the terror of race relations in contemporary London with naturalistic accuracy. Beneath the racial
"melting pot" rage fires of hostility that threaten to destroy
the moral fabric of the city. For instance, as Kate awaits the
train for her suburban hometown of Romley, where she ex-
pects to make connections with her past, she is temporarily
disoriented by the hate-filled slogans sprayed on the platform
walls: "NIGGERS GO HOME. KILL THE BLACK CUNTS WHO ARE
RUINING OUR COUNTRY. BRITS OUT OF NORTHERN IRELAND.
MUSLIM DOGS . . ." (105). The "shifting population" in *The
Ice Age*, which jarred Alison Murray's refined English sensibilities to the point where she could only ponder "who has so
undermined, so terrified, so threatened and subdued us?" (169),
reappears in *The Middle Ground* with a face and a name, along
with forceful resistance to its presence. Joseph Leroy, the
"black six-foot Rastafarian" (225), provides one example.
Drabble describes the working-class family of Irene Crowther,
Leroy's white girlfriend, who is in fact a lesbian, as no more
"violently anti-coloured" than the police who "manhandled"
Leroy's body after he was burned in a fire (239–40). Thinking
about the impending press coverage of the episode involving
Leroy, Evelyn, another casualty in the fire, does not expect
much from reporters who "loathed social workers as much as
they loathed unemployed blacks" (228). There is, of course,
Mujid, referred to by the omniscient narrator as "the Iraqi"
(81). He is summarily dismissed by Kate's friends even before
they meet him as "probably a terrorist" (83), an example of

the prevailing xenophobia that, ironically, spells near disaster for Evelyn when the ambulance requested after her accident is delayed because of the caller's Pakistani accent. At the end of the novel, Drabble attempts to impose some order on the straggly arrangement of social life in London by way of a Woolfian mainstay: a party. This postcolonial celebration differs significantly from its Edwardian counterpart both in tone and intent. For one thing Kate's party celebrates the novel's theme of "shapeless diversity" (230). As an amalgamation of four parties (Evelyn's "coming-out party, and Hugo's going-away party, and Mujid's going-away party and Mark's birthday party" [245]), the parent party signifies the postcolonial reality of border crossings. Evelyn leaves the hospital after a period of self-reflection on the social and racial injustices that plague the lives of persons like Leroy and Irene; Hugo and Mujid return "home" to the Middle East invigorated by their association with Kate and leaving parts of themselves with her as well; and Mark, at nineteen, moves a step beyond the threshold of a relatively stable adolescence into the uncertainty of postmodern life. Clarissa's party also stems from the desire to "assemble" (*Dalloway* 284), but here the gathering is not a patternless diversity but an exclusive club whose members belong to a confident monoculture.

Hugo's musings on the contemporary social scene in *The Middle Ground* capture the ideological distance between these two cultural performances: "Will any one ever again be able to write, with confidence, a book that assumes the significance of one culture only, will anyone ever again be able to stand *upright* in one nationality?" (173, emphasis added). One cannot help but recall Clarissa's redoubtably "upright" bearing in her all-British, self-privileging upper-class society, a reality her party is supposed to affirm. Kate, too, entertains notions of uprightness, as she tries to console herself and Hugo after each has summed up the other's strengths and failings: "Ah, well, at least we stay upright" (261). The statement which follows by way of an afterthought puts Drabble's use of the word in a context different from Woolf's: "Though . . . I sometimes think that if so many people weren't leaning on me, from different directions, I might fall over." Kate has a relational capacity that eluded Clarissa throughout her relationships. The effort that Kate and the other characters make to "stay upright" is a result of Drabble's desire to move beyond the cultural narrowness of Woolf's England, as well as the one she has inherited. That is why Evelyn Bennett, who shares the novel's limelight with Kate Armstrong, is able to sympathize with the severely burned yet maltreated Leroy, the man who nearly caused her face to be disfigured: "One did not have to be a saint," in Evelyn's view, "to feel pity for Joseph Leroy" (239).

Kate, on the other hand, reaches some level of understanding with Mujid, her Iraqi boarder, who painfully wrings from her an acknowledgment of her apathy towards, and ignorance of, other cultures. Mujid is transformed at the end from a tormentor who is both "an extra conscience and a pedagogue rolled into one" and "a refugee" she "must learn to love" (84,85) into a caring person. In the incident involving the abusive, eccentric Hunt, for example, Mujid refuses to go to bed until he has made certain Kate is safe. More importantly, Mujid is transformed from the unknown, exotic Other into an approximation of the familiar self: "in some curious way he had become a part of her own, for despite his situation and opinions, he was really as interested as anybody in the trivia of existence" (110). Releasing Mujid "from the grip of the representative" (229), Kate is free by the end of the novel to watch him and his fiancée, Simone, "stirring up their couscous" and see "a nice man" rather than "her idea of an Iraqi" (267). In this climate of tolerance even the bigotry of inebriated men like Hunt is taken seriously. In a conversation with Ruth about English schools, he laments the fact that "our common [read "Western"] culture is perishing" and then snipes at Ruth for "picking up black men in pubs" (273). This implicit exclusionism meets with Ruth's stiff rejoinder that in school "we did racism too" (274). Perhaps the reply is Drabble's way of informing the reader that English schools have begun to tackle the racial monster that is wreaking havoc in the society. "Different languages, different cultures, different history books": *The Middle Ground* is very far from reverse colonization but it does create a sense of foreboding (85). Drabble's concern for bridge-building extends beyond matters of race and ethnicity to include relations between the sexes. For example, after a painful separation from Ted, which throws Kate off an already tenuous balance, the two lovers are brought together again by Evelyn's injury and decide at the end to be civil to, if no longer in love with, each other. Evelyn, enduring a marriage that Ted honors more in letter than in spirit, actually enjoys a few minutes of conversation in bed with him as they recall a shared past neglected "so long that they'd forgotten part of it" (214). The spirit of compromise extends to Kate's view of Mujid and Simone; she is certain "domestic harmony" awaits them because they are willing to learn from each other. Mujid will pass on his tea-making skill to Simone and she, in turn, will polish his French.

The relationship between Kate and Hugo provides Drabble with a narrative opportunity to express her difficulty with and difference from Woolf. Modeled after Clarissa and Peter, Kate and Hugo parody Woolf's psychological gladiators and their mind games. Described in Drabble's intertext are echoes of the fractured bond between Peter and Clarissa (and, by inference, between Drabble and Woolf). A poignant passage toward the end of the novel illustrates Drabble's dialectical narrative method:

> "How lucky we are," said Kate still staring back, "that we should each think each other so wonderful." And she got up, and started to wipe the table, sweeping the crumbs carefully into her open palm, and Hugo, watching her, thought that sublime was indeed the word, for at such moments something in Kate seemed to shimmer just beneath or above the surface, *sub limen*, a breaking light, and she had this knack, this gift, for catching a little of it, but just within range, like an astral halo flickering on the sight, calling from him a corresponding gleam: a bright person, an angel in the house, among the crumbs and dustbins and

fish heads. Ah, folly, thought Hugo, as he watched, she is just a woman, and a rather gullible, foolish, self-centered, vain woman at that: and Kate, washing her hands under the rubber swizzle tap, looked back at Hugo, his delicate, intellectual ascetic features, so elegant, so precise, so firmly drawn, and thought, after all Hugo is only a man, a rather selfish, dangerous, and self-deluding one at that; with something effete, cruel even in the turn of his lip: poseur, a monkish poseur, and who knows what he has repressed and mutilated to achieve his nice balance? (P. 260)

This comedy of sexual manners comes with the full freight of Woolfian motifs: "an angel in the house," stream-of-consciousness, sexual and identity politics. Behind the grid of allusions Kate and Hugo serve as a comedic foil to Peter and Clarissa. The psychological sparring match, which recalls their predecessors' signature act, gains parodic force against the backdrop of an unglamorous existence. Woolf's Victorian "angel in the house," for example, now lives servantless "among the crumbs and dustbins and fish heads," her "gift" of charm (Clarissa's ecstasy) evidence by the "astral halo" that symbolizes the crowning achievement of a life of drudgery. Caught, like their Edwardian counterparts in a sex-free but sexually nuanced relationship, Kate and Hugo cut through their predecessor's elaborate evasions with matter-of-fact summations of each other ("she is just a woman" and "after all Hugo is only a man."), and redirect our gaze toward the important fact of their successful intergender alliance. For establishing and maintaining a lifeline across their complex psychological histories, Kate and Hugo can count their blessings (in Drabblean terms, their "luck").

For all Drabble's intentions to transcend racial, cultural, and sexual barriers in *The Middle Ground*, however, the overwhelming mood of the novel is at best "guardedly optimistic."[25] The effort toward optimism is undermined by a nihilism stemming from a belief in the "irrevocability of fate," a curious phrase in Drabblean teleology which means the luck of birth, that is, being born with physical, social, or intellectual advantages. In Drabble's universe, cultural or sexual amalgamation is stubbornly resisted by deterministic forces that set apart the lucky from the unlucky. Referring to herself as a "kind of Greek with a Greek view of the gods," Drabble is a firm believer in predestination; in her mind, to imagine "an individual destiny is really a form of hubris." She sees herself as having been given "a wonderful deal, a magnificent hand of cards,"[26] that is, the privilege of race, money, and education. This reality that our resources are not all equal is neither "fair" nor "right," Drabble muses, but she has acquiesced in it, lest she tempt the gods. The presence of fate's powerful hand in Drabble's fiction engenders a pervasive sense of futility in which even the most valiant effort at self-reconstruction or transcendence is bound to fail. Individuals are fixed in their allocated spaces by their sex, their past, or their characters, and in short, an irreversible fate: "You can't completely alter what you were given without doing yourself a great violence . . . ," Drabble tells Barbara Milton in an interview.[27]

Hence in *The Middle Ground*, whose title suggests, among other things, the need for rapprochement in a city teeming with difference, Drabble can come up with nothing "better than a pretence of belief" (250), "a conspiracy of faith" (224), in the effort to achieve cultural synthesis. It is significant in the novel that Evelyn Stennett, the kind and caring social worker who is a mender of broken lives, is the one who utters the message that contains not hope but "a working hypothesis": "We ought all to behave *as though* we trust one another . . ." (224). Trust is reduced to role-playing: "everyone must play a part in keeping whole the fabric: one must not panic, one must not run away, one must not spread alarm" (224), but one must definitely learn the art of pretense. Lying in a hospital bed amid an array of flowers, cards, and messages sent by well-wishers of all ages, temperaments, and hues, Evelyn is surprised that her accident has "unlocked a fund of good will" (241). However, this insight into the capability of the human consciousness to transcend self-interest is quickly blotted from Evelyn's mind and replaced by a mild form of pessimism:

"Why expect results, progress, success, a better society? All we can do is to join the ranks of the caring rather than the uncaring. All we can do in this world is to care for one another, in the society we have" (241).

For the womanist, "the society we have" is a social construction that should be rejected and demolished, not condoned and affirmed. The womanist project of reconstruction would eliminate the kind of neurosis that passes for caring in *The Middle Ground*. For instance, Kate's concern for the unlucky is a cover that hides her neurotic attraction to "hopeless cases" (116), and Evelyn, "the mildest of women," actually possesses a pathological fear and hatred of the old and frail (61). And what, in Kate's words, Hugo "has repressed and mutilated to achieve [his] nice balance" is a neglectful and obsessive mother who "had flirted with him rather than loved him" (122). The mature mother-son relationship is an absurdist comedy fit for the stage: "No culture gap there . . . rather a frightening amorous communion, a rapport so quick, so sharp, so intense, that an observer felt himself to be watching a pattern of courtship, a display . . . of mutual possession" (122). As Hugo thinks of his wife, Judith, and the way she has transformed caring for their brain-damaged son into a philosophy of revenge against hospital personnel responsible for the boy's condition, he rationalizes this bizarre predilection for self-disguise: "Love, they say, redeems, but it is itself that exposes us" (168). This impediment masquerading as affection is removed by womanist insistence on new, untangled beginnings.

Drabble's deterministic model of existence, however, vitiates the possibility of new beginnings. For women, in particular, biology is fate and as *The Middle Ground* demonstrates, not even the progress wrought by the feminist movement can relieve the burden of being female. In the novel Drabble depicts a problem-riddled feminist movement which has reached middle age and cannot figure out what the next step should be. Feminism's blessings are mixed; the price of liberation is costly. This is the underlying viewpoint of the novel and Kate

Armstrong's life provides a case study. A confident reaper of feminism's harvest—a lucrative career, the freedom to divorce, to choose multiple sexual partners, to abort, and to be a single parent, without the stigma once attached to these activities—Kate is nevertheless discontented. From experience, as well as from the stories of the women she interviews, Kate knows all too well that the feminist struggle against the elaborate systems designed to deny women's humanity is far from over, but she is not so disturbed by that fact as she is by the victories won. For her they are pyrrhic victories that have left her in disarray rather than in control.

The shaky ground on which Kate treads is symbolized by her wobbly boots, which constantly throw her off balance but never get fixed. She even confesses to Hugo that "for months I had this strange sensation, as if the world had in fact slipped, and I had fallen off it" (255). Kate is suffering from postfeminist trauma. She is caught between the rock of traditionalism and the hard place of liberation. Convinced that Stuart's "perverse instinct for self-destruction" (35) will hamper her progress, she quickly rids herself of him and focuses instead on her blossoming career. But she cannot shed as easily the ensuing guilt of the emasculating woman. She is certain that it is her "winning streak" that has engendered Stuart's "defeatist attitude." In the face of overwhelming evidence to the contrary— a bland premarital relationship, a hellish marriage, Stuart's lack of ambition—Kate still assumes all the blame for her husband's failure. She believes that she has in effect reversed the traditional male-female work roles and she finds the burden of her act unbearable.

The decision to abort a diseased fetus proves equally weighty for Kate. At forty, having passed the optimum child-bearing age, Kate had hoped the baby would restore the womanhood which she presumably lost after her children grew up. Little wonder then that Kate is teetering on the brink: nearly emptied of her reproductive self, she has little ground left to stand on. She needs to give birth to feel whole again. Aborting the spina bifida-infected fetus, Kate willingly undergoes sterilization, and thereby completes the process of her de-sexing which the abortion, in her view, has begun. The truth is that Kate is not only "sick to death" of women, who have been the primary subject of her journalistic career, she 'has had it' with *being* a woman or, better yet, the new woman, who is expected to savor the freedom of the present while she is still chained psychologically to a repressive past. The effects of this self-division in Kate border on the neurotic. Her obsessive need to be "nice," to seek victimization, is an extension of a bigger need to realize her maternal instinct, what she refers to as "her primary passion in life" (235). To replace an aborted baby she blames herself for murdering (an act she refers to in Clarissa-like fashion as "the death of a soul"), Kate finds surrogate babies in men, first the string of hopeless men she dates after the abortion and next, Hugo, her one-armed friend whom she literally feeds. Kate may have "cut out the child, but not the malady" (110).

The umbilical cord tying Kate to her past is also difficult to sever. A good deal of the dislocation she is experiencing in the present traces back to what the text refers to as her "heritage of sewage [and] agoraphobia" (26). Some of the effects of this heritage on Kate's current situation are easily discernible. For instance, her addiction to clutter is a gift from her sewage-loving father and her fear of flying links her with her agoraphobic mother. But the "imprint" of the Fletcher family "lay too heavy in her spirit" (12); it defied easy explanations. It needed a line of action that Drabble heroines such as Clara Maugham in *Jerusalem the Golden* and Frances Wingate in *The Realms of Gold* have taken in their quest for selfhood, namely, retrieving the past. The trip to Romley transports Kate to a psychological underworld of buried fears and fantasies. Kneeling down to sniff the odious sewage as she had done many times as a child is the act of confirmation she had been waiting for: she is without a doubt "her father's daughter" (120), which means she is heir to his neurotic attachment to slime and sludge and his unhealthy love of work. While she has known all along that her slovenly manner and nearly addictive work habits tied her to her father, she is forced to come to terms with the deeper ramifications of her inheritance—her untidy life, her attraction to scavengers like Hunt, and her inability to love in a sexual relationship. Kate traces the root of her performance-prone character to her deliberate attempt to cleanse her parents of their disgusting natures by "turn[ing] them into an acceptable version, in her own mind" (117). Her childhood game of "Confession" was in fact a sleight of hand, transforming socially offensive family traits into the stuff of comedy or, as she puts it, "turning shit into gold" (23). Her emotional paralysis, however, is proof that she failed to laugh away the problem.

Evelyn Stennett's surface serenity and reasonableness counterpoint Kate's dizzy hysteria but these too are a cover for the psychic brutality Evelyn is experiencing. Married and a working mother of adolescent children, Evelyn is Kate's double, her stable, middle-class origins set in direct opposition to Kate's nervous working-class background. But privileged Evelyn is as ensnared as self-made Kate. Trapped in a loveless marriage, Evelyn resorts to playing a game of her own: what I would call the rationalizing game. As postfeminist woman, Evelyn is supposed to handle her husband's infidelity intellectually; after all, freedom of choice does not seem to have spared the conjugal bed. But Ted's flagrant affairs, coupled with the knowledge that her husband has married her solely to boost his social standing ("they were an impressive package, the Morton sisters. . . . He'd done a clever thing in marrying Evelyn" [210]), are jarring enough to warrant a defense mechanism. By viewing their marriage as a favor done for an overly ambitious Ted, a gift for which he should be grateful (and "grateful he intermittently is, what more should I want?"), Evelyn is thus free to go beyond terminating sexual relations with her husband and enter the realm of befriending his lovers. Crossing that boundary is the ultimate test for the liberated married woman, one that presents Evelyn with a formidable challenge. A tell-tale sign of the ensuing difficulty is the "slope" she has created "on her side of the bed . . .

through years of effort spent keeping well away from Ted in the night" (214) for fear of yielding to her real feelings.

Such sexual repression, always a potent self-protective maneuver for Drabble's heroines (Emma in *The Garrick Year* and Jane in *The Waterfall*, for example), requires an even bolder stroke in Evelyn's case, given Ted's Darwinist philosophy of "survival of the fittest." Submission to sexual desire would be tantamount to self-sacrifice. Thus Evelyn settles for a damaged emotional life, rendered palatable by her oxymoronic dismissal of marriage as "a worn peacefulness," an "admirable cracked solidity" (149).

Drabble claims to have kept some distance between herself and Woolf "through fear and misunderstanding" until 1972 when she "stumbled upon *A Room of One's Own.*" In an essay published in *Ms.*, Drabble writes of how her discovery produced a fresh image of Woolf: not the "dull dilettante" who was "out of date, out of touch," but a "good fighter . . . braving the scorn of the majority" in her battle against patriarchy.[28] Drabble is also disappointed that the "brave new world of liberation" Woolf mapped out in her essays did not extend into her novels, which, as Drabble first thought, are "beautiful" but "irrelevant," an impression she tries to muffle by praising Woolf's ability to see with "a painter's eye." But Drabble's own fiction makes clear that she preferred the literary company of Arnold Bennett and Jane Austen to that of Woolf, or, as she would later put it, "I'd rather be at the end of a dying tradition which I admire than at the beginning of a tradition which I deplore."[29] As one concerned about social (some critics would say trendy) issues and an ardent admirer of Arnold Bennett, Drabble lays claim to the Victorian heritage of social and moral responsibility and rejects the self-conscious, language-dictated aesthetics of Woolf and her avant-garde contemporaries. Of course, given Woolf's open contempt for Bennett's brand of realism, coupled with her preference for androgynous rather than gender-restrictive writing, Woolf too may very well have found little to admire in Drabble.

The Middle Ground, written after Drabble had "discovered" Woolf, pokes fun at Woolf's upper-class world in *Mrs. Dalloway* by ending with a party which, in purpose, tone, and setting, is intended to contrast sharply with its predecessor. But Drabble is more attracted to Woolf than she would like to admit. Her attempts at parody in *The Middle Ground* belie a deep admiration for Woolf's undiminished concern about the debility of the modern condition. While several critics have noted the similarity between the two novels, Roberta Rubenstein makes the strongest case for *Mrs. Dalloway* serving as a source or, at least, an inspiration, for *The Middle Ground* when she describes the latter's plot as the story of

> a woman residing in London in the middle years of her life, reminiscing about the past and evaluating former relationships, including an important one with a person once quite close to her named Peter. She sometimes feels herself teetering on the edge of sanity, finds an affirmative sense of herself through (among other things) an accident that happened to someone else; in preparation for a party she will be giving later on a particular day goes to a florist shop to buy flowers. At the end of the novel she is the radiating center of relationships. The whole novel is told through an omniscient narrator who shifts the scenes among a central group of characters, with flashbacks to earlier experiences and relationships interwoven throughout the narrative.[30]

The omniscient narrator is, of course, a despised device in *Mrs. Dalloway* and Rubinstein's summary glosses over the convoluted pattern of events plotted in *The Middle Ground*. Nonetheless, she captures brilliantly the fact of intertextual engagement between the two novels. Drabble might also be influenced by Woolf's feminist ambivalence, as she, too, has disavowed any allegiance to feminist ideology, unconvinced by "the feminist view that there's a male conspiracy to put women down," believing instead that "the truth is more important than ideology."[31] In clinging to the traditional view that men lack ulterior motives in their relations with women, however, Drabble stands far afield from Woolf, who would

have been shocked that a Cambridge-educated woman familiar with the Enlightenment practice of sexual division favor-
ing men (as evidenced by Rousseau's *Emile*) could entertain
such thinking. As a liberal feminist, Woolf was all too aware
of the male determination to prevent women from achieving
personhood. She even went beyond the unconfrontational
liberal feminist stance of her predecessor, Mary Wollstonecraft, to mount a stinging attack (as the women-as-mirror
metaphor in *A Room of One's Own* reveals) against male tyranny. Yet while Woolf challenged the eighteenth-century legacy of philosophical devaluation of women, she could not re-
linquish its idea of a transcendent, unified rationality or the
attendant notion of a rarefied (and, Woolf insisted, androgynous) aesthetic. Thus the effort to render her creative mind
incandescent, not a lack of faith in feminist ideology, led
Woolf in her fiction to put narrative distance between herself
and her feminism.

On the other hand, Drabble sees the feminist struggle as a
distraction, at best (since in her mind, ideas about male conspiracy against women are grossly exaggerated) and at worst,
futile (because women were dealt an unlucky hand of cards
from the start). As late as 1986 Drabble was still defending her
non-feminist point-of-view. In *Contemporary Novelists* she writes:

> In this space I originally wrote that my books were mainly
> concerned with "privilege, justice and salvation," and that
> they were not directly concerned with feminism "because
> my belief in justice for women is so basic that I never think
> of using it as a subject. It is part of a whole." I stand by
> this, although the rising political consciousness of women
> has brought the subject more to the forefront in one or two
> of the later novels. I now see myself perhaps more as a so-
> cial historian documenting social change and asking ques-
> tions rather than providing answers about society: but my
> preoccupation with "equality and egalitarianism" remains
> equally obsessional and equally worrying to me, and if any-
> thing I am even less hopeful about the prospects of change.
> (P. 248).

This statement calls attention to the similarities and differences between Woolf and Drabble and, more importantly, between "womanist" Walker and "feminist" Drabble. In the first place, the latter's attempt to distance herself from a restrictive (and sullying) feminist realm is reminiscent of Woolf's effort to extricate women's and her own writing from the narrow sphere of gender-based artistic production. Woolf held strong and contradictory views on this subject, insisting in *A Room of One's Own*, on the one hand, that "it is fatal for anyone who writes to think of their sex" and on the other that "we think back through our mothers if we are women" (108,79). These twin ideas make strange bedfellows in Woolf's work, prompting a wide gamut of artistic responses ranging from the rhetorical murder of feminism in *Three Guineas* to the quintessential linguistic experiment of *The Waves*. Yet Woolf could not possibly conceive of Drabble's idea of "justice of women" being "so basic" (natural, predetermined?) as to defy literary concern. Nor does Walker, who opens up her white counterparts' gendered concept of justice to include other vistas of lived experience. Moreover, Walker's womanist strategy of confrontation replaces Drabble's existentialist doubt as a means to effect change.

Measured against the womanist paradigm of cultural cooperation, Drabble's conglomerate vision of English society represents a dramatic expansion of the narrow cultural vista provided in *Mrs. Dalloway*. The historical moments of these writers cannot, of course, be ignored. Woolf's England was awash in imperialist torrents, and traces of the accompanying debris of racial and class intolerance found their way into *Mrs. Dalloway*. There, as I argued in chapter 1, Woolf's characteristic rebelliousness clashed with a view of otherness that almost expresses, to borrow from Patrick Brantlinger's analysis of Victorian mythologization of Africa, "expresses a nostalgia for lost authority and for a pliable, completely subordinate proletariat. . . ."[32] Woolf's fictional distancing of the colonized Other, for instance, is, in large part, a reflection of the physical and cultural distance that separated England from its territories in the late nineteenth century.[33] In a post-Empire, postcolonial world, Drabble abandons Woolf's self-distancing tactics for an attitude that regards accommodation as a sensible alternative.

The Middle Ground represents Drabble's boldest effort to connect cultures and the sexes, but the effort remains unrealized. It is significant that Kate's party, the symbol of unity, is still, up to the end of the novel, only an idea and, without fruition, it lacks the moral force necessary to eradicate the predominant feeling that foreigners and women are, in Kate's words, "marginal people" in Drabble's England. Rubia Subhan, for example, the eight-year-old Pakistani girl, possesses more than the normal dose of fortitude and *joie de vivre* needed to guarantee happiness. But Rubia, "old before her time, a mother to her mother" (239), is already nipped in the bud. Her prospects for growth, much less full flowering, in the unnurturing environment of Drabble's England are dim, a reality confirmed by the ambulance episode in which her desperate cry for help is ignored because of her accent. Similarly, women in the novel are a deracinated bunch. Drabble deals a crushing blow to feminism, showing it as an additional burden to an already exacting female sexuality rather than the glory of achieved womanhood it is touted to be. For all of Woolf's feminist ambiguity, this is a position she would have considered extreme and Walker's celebration of a woman-centered world view in *The Color Purple* stands clearly in opposition to it.

3

The Color Purple

A STUDY OF WALKER'S
WOMANIST GOSPEL

Change means growth, and growth can be painful. But we sharpen self-definition by exposing the self in work and struggle together with those whom we define as different from ourselves. . . . For Black and white, old and young, lesbian and heterosexual women alike, this can mean new paths to our survival.

Audre Lorde, *Sister Outsider*

Womanism has brought Alice Walker and her characters safely to the land of psychic freedom after a perilous journey fraught with fear, self-hate, and guilt. The transforming agent (and transporting agency) is "womanish" gall, the courage to be daring in the face of a conspiracy of conformity and, if not silence, acquiescence. A traditionalist in the sense of one who believes in the authenticating capacity of orality, Walker locates womanism in the speech culture of black women. Being or "acting womanish," Walker writes, is "the folk expression" black female adults used to describe young girls who were overly curious, "audacious," and eager to enter the world of grown-ups'.[1] Womanishness is similar to, yet different from, its nonfolk correlative, precociousness. While both suggest prematurity or early ripening, the former takes on the added elements of willfulness and excessive curiosity, which are not necessarily a part of precocity. "Womanish," I think, links better with the West African pidgin expression "big woman" (pronounced "big ooman"), used also by adults (male and female, though it is female-derived) to refer to the sassy demeanor of young females. Since both expressions also provoke the contradictory response of disagreement over the young person's refusal to be circumscribed and tacit approval and admiration for the rebellious spirit, Walker's term, given the history of African retentions in African American folk culture, may very well have its origin in the West African version.

To distinguish further the black feminist writer from her white counterpart, Walker adds to the folk quality of reckless boldness, which she defines as "wanting to know more and in greater depth than is considered 'good' for one," the attributes of woman-centeredness (an appreciation or love of other women "sexually and/or non-sexually"), and a unified vision of the world. Couched in this definition of womanism is Walker's criticism of white liberal feminism, especially what she regards as its qualified resistance to the status quo and self-seeking amelioration in the face of massive global oppression. For Walker, the battle against patriarchal society and its multiple sins of sexism, racism, classism and homophobia (among others) needs the womanist spirit of defiance and irreverence, on the one hand, and the desire for social integration, on the other. Woolf's dialectics of resistance and compliance in *Mrs. Dalloway* and Drabble's deterministic model in *The Middle Ground* seem to justify Walker's unease with white feminism, yet a closer look at Walker's own feminist consciousness reveals a slow, torturous progress toward her emancipating womanist ethos. Walker's confident rebellion in *The Color Purple* is the culmination of a long struggle against despair, as well as racial and sexual fragmentation. The path to womanist victory in Walker's fiction is strewn with physically and psychically battered women, victimized as much by self-hate as by an oppressive racist and sexist social system.

In a 1973 interview Walker defined the subject of her creative imagination: "I am committed to exploring the oppressions, the insanities, the loyalties, and the triumphs of black women . . . the most fascinating creations in the world" (*Gardens*, 250–51). More precisely, the focus of Walker's attention is the Southern black woman and until *The Color Purple* her personal "oppressions" and "insanities" far out-numbered her "triumphs." The female characters in both Walker's first novel, *The Third Life of Grange Copeland*, and first collection of short stories, *In Love & Trouble*, are too close to their creator's near-suicide experience (involving an unwanted pregnancy in her final college year in 1965) to escape the mood of "completely numbing despair" that crisis engendered (*Gardens* 249). In *The Third Life of Grange Copeland* both male and female characters are caught beneath a brutally oppressive social machinery, but it is the women who are crushed by the double weight of racism and sexism. Grange Copeland tries to regain the manhood he lost to Shipley, the white man who "owned" him, by beating his wife, Margaret. Himself reduced to an object by Shipley, Grange in turn strips Margaret of her humanity, rendering her indistinguishable from "their dog."[2] Beaten and silenced, Margaret suffers alone, a silent sacrifice to brute masculinity. Not even in the murder of her unwanted child and her own suicide does Margaret show defiance. On the contrary, these acts, as Trudier Harris points out, "are a bow of defeat, a resignation," bearing the marks of one who, like a dog, "had spent the last moments on her knees" (21).[3]

In a second cycle of sadomasochistic violence, Brownfield and Mem repeat and expand the life-denying behavior of the earlier generation. Brownfield, aptly described by Bettye Parker-Smith as "a worm, a wretched, contemptible maggot," displaces his powerlessness within the dominant social structure onto women whom he treats with unrelieved venom.[4] Having sexually used and abused Josie (his father's mistress) and her daughter, Lorene, Brownfield reaches for the prize female, Mem, the superior woman with education and middle-class promise. Brownfield's gradual but certain destruction of Mem dramatizes the plight of black women vis-á-vis black men in a society that devalues blackness but privileges maleness. Mem and her fellow victims in *The Third Life* succumb to the guilt the black cultural economy produces to punish those women who fail to yield to male authority. Feeling partly responsible for white society's emasculation of black men, these women offer themselves in atonement, their self-sacrifice demanding from them total submission to male desire. This religion of submission, the driving force in the lives of Walker's early female characters, earns Mem the title of "saint," the dubious honor accorded her by Grange, her husband's father, for her incredible feat of self-erasure. Mem's pathological passivity shocks the sensibilities. Advantaged by education and class, she chooses nonetheless to put herself in the service of an illiterate reprobate who gets his kicks from cutting her down to manageable size. Brownfield strips Mem of her language (forcing her to drop her "damn proper" idiom for "talk like the rest of us poor niggers"), her claim to her own body (by continuously beating and impregnating her), and, finally, her being (by murdering her). Like Margaret, Mem is no better than "an old no-count dog," deprived of the will to fight back by an urge to make Brownfield "feel a little bit like a man" (94). The overwhelming sense of female victimization that permeates *The Third Life of Grange Copeland* is most likely one of the reasons why Walker called it "a grave book" (*Gardens*, 263). Despite her inclusion of Ruth, the third-generation female who projects the self-confidence of a later day, Walker does not escape the cultural guilt economy that trades black female identity for black male gratification.

The theme of thwarted black female identity continues in the short stories of *In Love & Trouble*. Here, too, the twin scourges of sexism and racism beat women to their knees where they remain, hopeless supplicants before a mercilessly brutal social structure. "Her Sweet Jerome" offers a haunting example of female self-destruction. Mrs. Jerome Franklin Washington III, referred to throughout the story as "she" (except for the one instance in which she calls herself by the coveted marital name), embodies the principle of self-negation.

Lacking a name of her own, she has no recourse to an identity separate from her role as wife, a position she won only after a Herculean show of effort and which she is determined to keep at any cost. Not surprisingly, news that "her cute little man is sticking his finger into somebody else's pie" sends her reeling from her precarious perch into madness and death.[5] By the time her frenzied search for her husband's lover ends in the shocking discovery of a pile of books rather than another woman, Mrs. Jerome Franklin Washington III has not only lost her reason but has transmogrified into a beast: "Her firm bulk became flabby. Her eyes were bloodshot and wild. She smelled bad from mouth and underarms and elsewhere . . . she has taken to grinding her teeth and tearing at her hair as she walked along" (29–30). In the end, as she burns her determined and contingent self out of existence, the effect is not pathos but relief.

Marriage as entrapment is also the theme in "Roselily," a story of deep psychological turmoil framed by a seemingly benign social transaction. Roselily is getting married and upon the culture-bound text of wedding vows she inscribes her own text, one that indicts at once her culture for its offer of marriage as women's salvation and herself for believing in the efficacy of that idea. In her interior monologue we find Roselily's real story, the tale of a life crippled by loneliness, poverty, back-breaking labor, and the desperate search for escape. Rescue for this mother of four comes in the form of marriage to a man whose manner and religion spell domination. The married space, filled with images of her veiled face and promises of more babies, will be, as Roselily rightly intuits, just as confining as her beleaguered past. It will not allow her "to live for once" (8) and yet it is her only chance at "respect" for herself and her children. As with Mem, there are intimations of a rebellious spirit in Roselily, manifested, for instance, in the desire "to strike [the preacher] out of the way, out of her light, with the back of her hand" (8). But the blow is directed instead at herself in the final scene where, in a significant shift to an omniscient narrative perspective, we are shown Roselily, cowed and "feel[ing] ignorant, *wrong,* backward" (9) as she walks behind her husband into a second round of bondage.

The female character in "Really Doesn't Crime Pay?" acts as spoil for two men: her husband, who married her only because her brown skin is the closest thing to the real but unattainable object of his desire, a white woman; and her lover, a phoney artist and plagiarist. The narrator (it is not clear if the name "Myrna," which appears in parenthesis below the title, is hers) is one of those silent and unsung black female artists Walker would later celebrate in the womanist prose of "In Search of Our Mothers' Gardens," but for now the character is a willing accomplice to the rape of her mind and body. For Ruel (her husband), she is a sex object to be made perpetually desirable with preening, perfumes, and lotions. Her "sweetened . . . body" is his play thing. Mordecai Rich, too, uses her body but it is her creative mind that serves him better. A writer without words of his own, he steals her story, publishes it in his name, and leaves town. Madness is the logical consequence of this symbolic silencing, and as the narrator attempts to saw off her husband's head in his sleep, it is clear that protest and resistance must replace passivity if the black woman is to survive. Her husband's murder averted, the narrator, therefore, finds another death-dealing act of protest: the birth-control pills she swallows "religiously" each day will certainly kill Ruel's chances for the children he so desperately wants. And in the end when she is "quite, quite tired of the sweet sweet smell of [her] body," she "will leave him . . . forever without once looking back" (23).

Such signs of budding resistance in *In Love & Trouble* are few but their very presence amidst the intractable oppressive forces that govern the lives of these women suggests that their author is contemplating a re-evaluation. Walker's "personal historical view of Black women," notes Mary Helen Washington, "sees the experiences of Black women as a series of movements from a woman totally victimized by society and by men to a growing, developing woman whose consciousness allows her to have control over her life."[6] Clearly, the goal of female self-understanding is not a crucial component of Walker's aesthetics in either *The Third Life of Grange Copeland* or *In Love & Trouble;* instead, these works mark, in Walker's trajectory of black womanhood, the mule-of-the-world stage in the development of black female consciousness. Lowest in the hierarchy of white and male social privilege, Walker's early women are, to use Washington's apt word, "suspended," caught between sexism and racism. This angle of Walker's artistic vision sheds light on her decision to expunge from the final version of *The Third Life of Grange Copeland* a first draft which "began with Ruth as a Civil Rights lawyer in Georgia going to rescue her father, Brownfield Copeland, from a drunken accident, and to have a confrontation with him" (*Gardens* 255). Such a beginning would have opened the window on an entirely different view of womanhood, the kind that will reach full flowering in *The Color Purple* but is only slowly emerging on the pages of *The Third Life of Grange Copeland* and *In Love & Trouble.*

The new strain of black femaleness we get a peek at appears not only in Ruth (who, in her historically "correct" place as a third-generation woman, begins to claim the lost voice of her predecessors) but also in the weather-beaten women of *In Love & Trouble.* Like the powerful example of female subterfuge via denial of fertility in "Really, Doesn't Crime Pay?" the title character in "The Revenge of Hannah Kemhuff" exacts a heavy price from her white oppressor. When Sara Marie Sadler denies Hannah the chance to feed her starving self and children during the hunger-filled Depression simply because she looked neat in her hand-me-down clothes, Hannah loses everything she values: her children, her pride and hope, and her life. But with the last ounce of energy left in her withered body, she turns Tante Rosie's root-working magic on Sarah to make sure that her enemy is deprived of the right to exist, too. Hannah's revenge is a mild but potent act of self-affirmation; like the young woman who disobeys her father's command to give up her white lover in "The Child Who Favored Daughter," a refusal for which she pays with her life, or like the mother who rejects her daughter's new-found ideology of solipsism in "Everyday Use," Hannah is a harbinger of the reconstituted image of black womanhood found in Walker's later fiction.

Walker has criticized white American writers for "end[ing] their books and their characters' lives as if there were no better existence for which to struggle." Unlike black writers who strive toward "some kind of larger freedom," white writers, she says, tend to thick[en]" their writings with the "gloom of defeat" (*Gardens* 5). Of course, she is quick to point to the generalized character of her observation, noting that the comparison "perhaps does not really hold up at all" (*Gardens* 6). Walker's rethinking on this matter may have something to do not only with the weakness of her comparison but also with the suspicion that her own fiction, especially in its early stages, is as painful as, say, Faulkner's or O'Connor's. Her movement toward the womanist optimism of *The Color Purple* can be seen as simultaneously an acknowledgment and a rejection of the lure of defeat that permeates *The Third Life of Grange Copeland* and *In Love & Trouble.*

While Walker considers concrete experience invaluable to the creative process (many of her characters, including Celie, have real-life analogues and some of her stories are renditions of her mother's tales—part of her effort to legitimatize the black female experience), she also believes, with Camus, that "though all is not well under the sun, history is not everything" (*Gardens* 21). But the re-creation of history *is*, for it allows "connections [to be] made . . . where none existed before, the straining to encompass in one's glance at the varied world the common thread, the unifying theme through immense diversity, a fearlessness of growth, of search, of looking, that enlarges the private and the public world" (*Gardens* 5). And so after capturing the poignant but narrow vista of recollected scenes from her native South in *The Third Life of Grange Copeland* and *In Love & Trouble*, Walker positions her creative lens for what she believes to be the hallmark of art,

"the larger perspective" (*Gardens* 5). *The Color Purple* is the site
of this diffuse creative activity but first the path must be cleared
through *Meridian.*

Midway between despair and hope, *Meridian* is a novel that
meets life at the cross-roads and agonizes over the road to be
taken. Meridian Hill, the main character, is a curious amal-
gam of the traditional female of Walker's early fiction and the
liberated woman of her later work. How to become the latter,
that is, a self-constituting being, is the essence of her story.
Meridian must claw her way through layers of culturally induced guilt to reach a convincing plateau of selfhood, a feat
that paralyzes both her will and body and barely lifts her
above empty despair. First is the guilt she must carry because
her mother is not "a woman who should have had children."[7]
An ambitious and self-motivating woman, Meridian's mother
in her early adulthood had embraced motherhood in order to
find out the tantalizing secret behind the "mysterious inner
life" of "the mothers of her pupils," women who seemed to
have found contentment in the drudgery of their lives. What
she discovered after six children was that her imaginings
about these women had lured her siren-like into motherhood,
a cultural institution that insists on female self-negation. It
was not "euphoria" that gave these mothers the contented
look, as Meridian's mother had previously surmised, but,
rather a mind-binding pain carefully concealed from the
world's judgment. Like them, having lost all claim to selfhood, "she was not even allowed to be resentful" (40). The
effect was the feeling of "being buried alive, walled away
from her own life, brick by brick" (41); perishing in the
process were her creativity and all traces of affection for all
children, especially her own. Thus, "for stealing her mother's
serenity, for shattering her mother's emerging self . . .
Meridian felt guilty from the very first" (41).

Meridian's second wave of guilt stems from the first: to
prevent her son from robbing her of her own life, Meridian
gives him away. Convinced that her act has saved two lives—
hers and her son's, both of which she had wanted to terminate

—Meridian is nonetheless wracked by "an almost primeval guilt" (92) sanctioned by that stern, unyielding cult known as "Black Motherhood" (93), whose tradition of self-sacrifice her mother had personified and Meridian now betrays by abandoning her son. The communal voice of condemnation, one that Shug Avery in *The Color Purple* would later simply ignore, follows her to Saxon College where she "curs[ed] her existence . . . that could not live up to the standard of motherhood that had gone before" (88). But as thoughts of suicide give way to active participation in the struggle for racial equality, Meridian begins to see a larger picture, one in which her act of betrayal, as well as the monument of black motherhood, pales beside the terrible reality of racial hatred.

The larger perspective provided by Saxon College and the civil rights movement also brings with it some self-understanding for Meridian.[8] Her fear of sex, for instance, which had manifested itself earlier in her relationship with Eddie, her son's father, resurfaces in her brief romance with Truman as tangible evidence that she does not fill the stereotype of woman as object of male sexual gratification. Meridian had resisted Eddie, a man she did not love, with legs that looked "like somebody starched them shut" (57). Truman seems to stand a better chance because with him she "felt she had discovered a missing sense" that she can gratify through "hot, quick, mindless" love-making with him (96). But sex with Truman turns out to be as mechanical as it was with Eddie; her mind oversees the process with vigilance and deliberation. Once again, the sex act leaves her unfulfilled and pregnant. This time, however, her speedy termination of both the pregnancy and the relationship with Truman point to an emerging sense of self as subject. When Truman returns to her with the directive, "*Have* my beautiful black babies," Meridian hears the male voice of authority that in an earlier time had blocked the growth of Margaret and Mem Copeland, and she reacts with swift vengeance:

And she drew back her green book bag and began to hit him. She hit him three times before she even knew what was happening. Then she hit him again across the ear and a spiral from a tablet cut his cheek. Blood dripped onto his shirt. When she noticed the blood she turned and left him to the curiosity of the other students crowding there. (p. 113)

With this blood-letting ritual, Meridian posits herself as subject rather than object, but this act of hegemonic reversal proves costly. Retribution comes in the form of alienation and psychic disorientation. Her tenuous relation with the black community (she finds the God of the black church, for instance, incomprehensible), coupled with her lack of positive female role models (except for her father's grandmother, Feather Mae, whose religion of "physical ecstasy" she hopes to inculcate), assists her slide into voluntary solitariness. But even from here, Meridian intends to engage the world on her own terms. One-by-one she sheds the features of male-structured identity—status, material comfort, romantic love, respect for the law—for a self-definition located in challenge and self-sacrifice.

As Meridian throws her starved and emaciated body in front of an army tank in an effort to prevent school children from viewing the body of Marilene O'Shay, murdered by her jealous husband, or as she comforts Lynne Rabinowitz, the woman Truman married and has abandoned to return to the love he thinks he and Meridian shared, it is obvious that the logic of her self-identity defies conventional thinking on womanhood. As Anne Marion terminates her friendship with Meridian, she captures the sense of bafflement and misunderstanding that Meridian's problematic new self provokes: "Meridian, I can not afford to love you. Like the idea of suffering itself, you are obsolete" (124). This remark is only half-true. That side of Meridian that insists on self-punishment is obviously obsolete, for it is a throwback to a time when women like Margaret or Mem Copeland cast themselves as willing victims. But there is another side to Meridian: that which has engendered an alternative economy of selfhood, namely the will to act on her own behalf. As if unable to withstand the weight of this momentous act of defiance, Meridan's (female) body literally disintegrates after it is taken over by a mysterious disease referred to only as "her illness" (144). But it is a bold spirit that chafes beneath the husk that remains to her, a spirit strengthened by a new self-concept: "For she understood, finally, that the respect she owed her life was to continue, against whatever obstacles, to live it, and not to give up any particle of it, without a fight to the death, preferably *not* her own" (204). Here, indeed, is the blueprint for the brave new world to be ushered in *The Color Purple*.

You Can't Keep A Good Woman Down, Walker's second collection of short stories, serves as a test site for the theme of female liberation. But a disproportionate emphasis on such trendy aspects of the women's movement as pornography, abortion, and rape gives these stories a thick polemical flavor, relieved neither by the thematic richness of *In Love & Trouble* nor the subtle complexity of *Meridian*. With such titles as "How Did I Get Away with Killing One of the Biggest Lawyers in the State? It Was Easy," "Porn," "The Abortion," and "You Can't Keep a Good Woman Down," Walker not only captures the prevailing mood of the times but also seems intent that the psychological distance between the free spirits in this collection and their fettered predecessors from *In Love & Trouble* will not go unnoticed. In "The Abortion" the protagonist's attitude toward the self/other dichotomy, previously a burden for Walker's female characters, speaks to the topical character (as well as the undecorated literalness) of these stories. Lying in a recovery room after aborting her child, Imani intones: "Well . . . it was you or me, Kiddo, and I chose me."[9] Self-abnegation is a thing of the past for this group of women and they make no bones about it.

If female autonomy as represented in *You Can't Keep a Good Woman Down* has an aesthetically grating effect, in *The Color Purple* it receives its finest artistic expression, mainly because it is conjoined with another cherished idea of Walker's, namely, life as a harmonious whole. In the essay "Saving the Life That Is Your Own" Walker writes: "It has been said that

someone asked Toni Morrison why she writes the kind of
books she writes, and that she replied: 'Because they are the
kind of books I want to read.' This remains my favorite reply
to that kind of question.'"[10] *The Color Purple*, then, like Morrison's *Sula*, is a book Walker had to write. Indeed it is a book
toward which she had been philosophically orienting herself
throughout her writing career.

Two habits of thought led Walker irreversibly to *The Color
Purple:* an insatiable curiosity that borders on rebelliousness,
and an unshakable belief in the interrelatedness of the multi-
farious strands of existence. Walker's essays provide valuable
insight into these shaping forces. Regarding her penchant for
the curious, she writes: "Curiosity is my natural state and has
led me headlong into every worthwhile experience (never mind
the others) I have ever had" (*Gardens* 366). Apart from engendering a desire for exploration (resulting in trips to Africa,
Cuba, China, Europe, Zora Neale Hurston's grave site, and
the homes of Flannery O'Connor and William Faulkner),
Walker's curious mind is also drawn to what Barbara Christian calls "the forbidden."[11] Taboo has always held a fascination for Walker because it means another challenge that she
must meet. In college, for instance, confronted with the law
prohibiting racial mixing, social and genetic, Walker recalls
in *Living by the Word* that she responded in characteristic fashion: "I actively combatted it by having numerous friendships
with white women and children, and by dating white men. I
later married, had a child by, and divorced a white man."[12]

Walker's curiosity is an integral element in her quest for
truth. Dissatisfied with the limited vision of existing systems
of knowledge, she feels the need for a new truth, one that will
come about "only . . . when all the sides of the story are put
together, and all their different meanings make one new one"
(*Gardens* 49). This re-made story will affirm the oneness or
"wholeness" of life, the connectedness of all living forms.
With the intensity of a Romantic, Walker has managed to
turn the idea of the unity of nature into a personal religion.[13]
It permeates her poetry and prose. Commenting on the rela-

tions between Blacks and Jews, for example, she writes: "Every affront to human dignity necessarily affects me as a human being on the planet, because I know every single thing on earth is connected" (*Gardens* 353). Walker's neo-pantheistic message of the "world [as] God" and "full humanity . . . [as] a state of oneness with all things" (*Gardens* 265) reaches evangelistic heights in the essay "The Universe Responds," in which she sums up an account of a stray dog with this evocation:

> I think I am telling you that the animals of the planet are in desperate peril, and that they are fully aware of this. No less than human beings are doing in all parts of the world, they are seeking sanctuary. But I am also telling you that we are connected to them at least as intimately as we are connected to trees. Without plant life human beings could not breathe. Plants produce oxygen. Without free animal life I believe we will lose the spiritual equivalent of oxygen. "Magic," intuitions, sheer astonishment at the forms the Universe devises in which to express life—itself—will no longer be able to breathe in us. (*Living*, 192)

The human link in this ecological chain of being is of particular concern to Walker. It is humans, in her view, who pose a threat to the chain because of their proclivity for fragmentation: "Everything around me is split up, deliberately split up. History split up, literature split up, and people are split up too. It makes people do ignorant things" (*Gardens* 48). Walker sees an irony in this separatist tendency, based on her contention that genetically pure individuals or racial groups are a rarity. She cites her own mixed ancestry—African, Cherokee, Indian, and white—as an example of the inherently heterogeneous characteristic of human beings, and decries America's reluctance to come to terms with its consanguinity as the root cause of its spiritual dis-ease:

> One of the reasons our country seems so purposeless (except where money is concerned) is that Americans, even (and perhaps especially) genetically, have been kept from acknowledging and being who they really are. There are

fewer "white" people in America, for instance, and even fewer "black" ones. This reality is a metaphor for countless other areas of delusion. In our diversity we have been one people—just as the peoples of the world are one people— even when the most vicious laws of separation have forced us to believe we are not. (*Living*, 128)

Womanist ideology, therefore, born out of Walker's insistence on new ways of perceiving self and other, is not revisionist, but revolutionary. Its goal is change and its target the "splits" of race, sex, and class that divide humanity. *The Color Purple*, which enacts this revolutionary vision, is the kind of book that, according to Christine Froula, Woolf in 1931 had predicted would emerge from the female unconscious, but only after fifty years.[14] Although Walker assigns *The Color Purple* to the genre of historical novel, the text works more to subvert rather than exemplify that male-identified category. In a clever literary move, Walker utilizes the traditional historical model only to explode it. Rape, racial and sexual oppression, and colonialism position themselves in the novel as cultural imperatives to give the impression of business as usual. However, slowly but persistently these structures are undermined and by the end of the novel their raison d'etre has been totally invalidated and supplanted by the foundations of a moral imperative. As Froula accurately points out, *The Color Purple* "undoes the patriarchal cultural order and builds upon new ground."[15]

One of the pillars of the patriarchal stronghold brought down in the novel is the idea of woman as marginal. In the beginning of the novel, Celie, the fourteen-year-old protagonist, is locked within a cultural text that defines her as an object. Raped, beaten, silenced, and sold into marital slavery by the man she thinks is her father, Celie begins to doubt her humanity, and as her debasement continues in the hands of Mr. _____, she actually entertains thoughts of self-erasure: "He beat me like he beat the children . . . I make myself wood. I say to myself, Celie, you a tree. That's how come I know trees fear man."[16] Rendered nonhuman by patriarchal law, Celie is deprived even of the self-protective mechanism of anger, a right every human being exercises in the event of an assault to her/his personhood. Listening to Sofia's personal narrative of the justifiable use of anger, Celie responds:

> I can't even remember the last time I felt mad . . . I used to get mad at my mammy cause she put a lot of work on me. Then I see how sick she is. Couldn't stay mad at her. Couldn't be mad at my daddy cause he my daddy. Bible say, Honor father and mother no matter what. Then after while every time I got mad, or start to feel mad, I got sick. Felt like throwing up . . . Then I start to feel nothing at all. (P. 47)

Celie's inscription as object is at once metaphoric and literal.

Embedded within this cultural text, however, is a subtext that reveals Celie as patently human and female. Far from being "dumb," as her Pa has labeled her, Celie is intelligent, perceptive and creative. For instance, even though she is too young to understand the full implications of her rape by Pa, she knows enough to steer her sister, Nettie, away from a similar fate. Further, during an accidental encounter with Olivia, the infant daughter whom Pa gave away, Celie's innate intelligence allows her to immediately recognize her own child. In addition, Celie possesses a creative core that manifests itself not only in quilt-making but also in a poetic imagination. Shug's flamboyance, for example, inspires Celie to write that "she look so stylish it like the trees all around the house draw themself up for a better look" (50). And later, trying to capture the wicked side of Shug's personality, Celie notes, "But evil all over her today. She smile, like a razor opening" (60). Harpo's despondency over his inability to tame Sofia is conveyed with the same richness of metaphor: "Harpo sit on the steps acting like he don't care. . . . He look out toward the creek every once in a while and whistle a little tune. But it nothing compared to the way he usually whistle. His little whistle sound like it lost way down in a jar, and the jar in the bottom of the creek" (69). Celie's gift for words is evident throughout the text. Her letters bear the imprint of a keen, perceptive mind, one that is capable of interpreting (not just documenting) reality.[17]

Also contrary to the predominating cultural text, Celie is sexually alive. As a victim of extended rape—first by Pa and then by Albert, who "go[es] to the toilet on [her]"—she is expected to be drained of any sexual desire of her own (79). Indeed, her premature menopause, probably induced by the trauma of sexual abuse, is read as a symbol of her de-sexing. In the minds of Pa and Mr. _____, Celie is neither a man nor, devoid of her periods, a woman. Therefore, for Pa she is a beast of burden that is auctioned off to the first bidder, and for Mr. _____, who purchases her, she is a sperm repository. But far from being sexually inert, Celie is ripe with desire to be spent not on a man ("I don't even look at mens," she confesses [15]) but on Shug Avery ("The most beautiful woman I ever saw" [16]). Shug's picture excites her and she almost loses control while bathing Shug's sick but tantalizing body: "First time I got the full sight of Shug Avery long black body with it black plum nipples, look like her mouth, I thought I had turned into a man" (53). But unlike a man who at such a moment would most likely think of rape, the supreme act of female devaluation, Celie raises physical desire to the level of the spiritual: "I wash her body, it feel like I'm praying. My hands tremble and my breath short" (53). The fact is that though in the patriarchal sexual economy Pa can describe Celie as no longer "fresh" (17), according to Shug, she is "still a virgin" (79), and making love to Shug is tantamount to her first sexual act. That Celie's sexuality, like her humanity, can remain intact under a prolonged male siege is evidence that contradicts and invalidates her dominant image as pathological victim.

Celie's transgressive act of desire puts into proper prospective Clarissa's furtive lesbianism in *Mrs. Dalloway*. The similarities in the sexual geographies of these women are so striking as to reward the effort to distinguish between their attempts to establish a radical sexuality. Like Celie, Clarissa incarnates a homoerotic force threatened to be contained by marriage and motherhood, both of which act as encroachments that wreak havoc on their bodies; Clarissa is left pale and weak by influenza and Celie enters early menopause. Ironically, the heterosexist configuration is broken with the birthing process, reconfirming the virginity of both women. Clarissa "could not dispel a virginity preserved through childbirth which clung to her like a sheet" (46) and Celie is said to be "still a virgin" (79) after two children with Pa and sexual experiences with Mr. _____ during which she renders herself invisible. Sexually revived, Celie convincingly resists patriarchal reappropriation, as she settles in a libidinal economy in which coupling is for pleasure. On the contrary, Clarissa's expression and subsequent denial of her passion for Sally Seton, begins the process by which she sees her (sexual) self through the distorting lense of convention. As "the perfect hostess" (9), Clarissa is locked into a vicious matrix of libidinal renunciation and maintenance of a sexless class order, a sado-masochistic act symbolized by her sheathed (and sheeted, postnatal) virginity. Accorded the same sexual advantage, Celie and Clarissa make different choices that betray their (and their creators') differing relations to the patriarchal order.

In the textual configuration of sexual politics, Sofia and Shug abandon Meridian's subterfuge and Celie's subtlety for the tactics of confrontation. Armed with a self-definition that defies male-determined social categorization, Sofia and Shug claim the center as the space to enact their humanity, vigorously resisting any attempt to be pulled into the margins. Having cut her way through layers of male intransigence, Sofia, for instance, believes she has earned her place in the center: "All my life I had to fight. I had to fight my daddy. I had to fight my brothers. I had to fight my cousins and my uncles. A girl child ain't safe in a family of men" (46). And in the extended "family of men," Harpo, Sofia's husband, intends to keep her under male tyranny. But his attempt, inspired by his father's example, is met with swift retaliation: "Next time us see Harpo his face a mess of bruises. His lip cut. One of his eyes shut like a fist. He walk stiff and say his teef ache" (43). Clearly, the taming of Sofia is not as easy as Harpo had been led to think.

Shug Avery is equally unmalleable; in her case no one has dared pin her down to a preconceived idea of her identity because in word and deed she is determined to remain unshackled. She embodies the truth contained in her advice to Celie: "You have to git man off your eyeball, before you can see anything a'tall" (179). Shug does not compartmentalize reality. Rather, she sees it as a continuum that in its capaciousness allows her to love (sexually) man and woman, victim and victimizer (Celie and Albert); to relegate the care of her children to someone else without feeling guilty (unlike Meridian or Woolf's Clarissa); and to conceive of God as "everything . . . that is ever was or ever will be" (178). Shug, like Morrison's Sula, "has been endowed with dimensions of other possibility" and therefore "whatever she is, is a matter of her own choices."[18] This is the state of selfhood that Meridian aspired toward but could not attain because the scapegoat mentality that derives from female secondariness (the type Kate Armstrong exhibited in her obsessive desire to please) undermined her potential.

Unburdened by guilt or any of the cultural strictures designed to constrain women, Shug is the quintessential free spirit. She sees nothing wrong, for instance, in liking Anna Julia and at the same time hurting her by stealing her husband (Albert). And if she can share Albert with Celie, why should she not share Celie with Albert? Although falling in love with nineteen-year-old Germaine, a "child . . . a third of my age" (221), scares Shug as much as it jolts Celie, it is another experience that has been dropped on Shug's path and she will not walk away from it. Multiple, even chaotic, experience is her domain.[19] She sums up her liberationist philosophy in her response to Albert's declaration that society will condemn Celie if she abandons her housekeeping chores and runs off to Memphis: "Why any woman give a shit what people think is a mystery to me" (182). Other not-so-bold women rally around this battle cry: Celie finally breaks out of her cocoon with self-prophesying words: "I'm pore, I'm black, I may be ugly and can't cook . . . But I'm here" (187), and Mary Agnes expresses herself in song and with Grady, Shug's husband. It is clear from these acts of self-affirmation that Walker is moving us from one reality into another.

In Walker's womanist universe the collapse of male-erected boundaries that separate woman from her self is a necessary first step toward coalition-building. Women must themselves be whole before they can be part of a wholeness. Speech or the end of silence is the key marker of female selfhood. As bell hooks puts it, "Silence is the condition of one who has been dominated, made an object; talk is the mark of freeing, of making one subject."[20] With their voice no longer dammed up, women's creativity, which before appeared in trickles, explodes, and in the place of "sister's choice," the quilt Celie was unsure she and Sofia could perfect, we have a human quilt in which segmented realities of sex, race, and culture are woven into one, unbroken pattern. Celie, for example, exercises the power of voice by speaking the truth to Albert, who had silenced her and hid Nettie's letters away from her. "Until you do right by me," she tells him, "everything you touch will crumble" (187). And as Celie's and Albert's fates take different turns—Celie flourishing both creatively and financially in Folkspants, Unlimited, her Memphis-based business, while Albert wallows in filth and lassitude—it is clear that Celie's "curse" has a moral authority that must be reckoned with. Albert's gradual understanding of the new dispensation of peaceful coexistence releases him from "meanness" that "kill[s]" (201) into a human community of love where he learns that life is something to be enriched, not diminished. He revives his sewing talent, which has been buried under years of masculine posturing, becomes an avid shell collector, participates in the communal feeding of yam to Henrietta, who needs it to combat a rare blood disease, and learns to listen. Albert sums up his transformation in a conversation with Celie: "I'm satisfied this the first time I ever lived on Earth as a natural man. It feel like a new experience" (230). "Natural" man, in Walker's cosmology, has shed his gender-based superiority complex and is ready to coexist with "natural" woman, who no longer sees herself as inferior.

If Celie's voice is instrumental in the resolution of sexual difference, Sofia's plays a key role in bridging the racial gap. Against life-threatening odds, Sofia claims her right to speech as she defends her humanity against a remark from the mayor's wife and her body from assault by the mayor. These two bigots share a racial ideology designed to keep Sofia in eternal serfdom as surely as Albert's sexist mentality held Celie in vassalage. Sofia is savagely beaten, imprisoned, and confined to servitude in the mayor's household, the very fate she had tried to resist. As her instinct for revenge simmers down and she slowly repairs her voice, Sofia feels it is time to set the racial record straight. The occasion for speaking the truth presents itself through Eleanor Jane, the mayor's daughter, who admits to her husband that "Sofia raise me, practically" (231). When Eleanor Jane demands of Sofia a confession of love for her son, Reynolds Stanley Earl, she is in fact asking is for Sofia to dismiss the feelings of hurt and humiliation that have built up over a period of eleven-and-a-half years of servitude and, instead, to embrace her oppressors as though they were her benefactors. This reality is not lost on Sofia and she responds appropriately: "No ma'am . . . I do not love Reynolds Stanley Earl." Pressed further, she adds, "I don't feel nothing about him at all. I don't love him, I don't hate him" (233). When Eleanor Jane accuses her of being "unnatural" and unlike "the other colored women [who] love children," Sofia hammers back with an even more painful truth: "I love children . . . But all the colored that say they love yours is lying" because they can no more love their oppressor, which is what young Reynolds will become when he grows up, than they can "the cotton gin," the symbol of their oppression (233).

This exchange between the races, like its sexual counterpart between Celie and Albert, is a necessary preamble to Walker's new constitution, which seeks a peaceful cohabitation of human beings. It clears the air for the settling of differences, because the point Sofia hopes to get across to Eleanor Jane is that although she has been ground down by her oppressors, she has shown a great deal of humanity by the mere fact that she harbors no hate for them. Asking her for love, therefore, is a thinly disguised act of subjugation because it denies Sofia the right to anger as surely as she had earlier been denied the right to speech. Eleanor Jane must have gotten the message, because by the end of the novel she, like Albert, has broken away from self-concern to participate in the urgent matter of feeding Henrietta the life-saving yam diet. And for the unconverted who ask, "Whoever heard of a white woman working for niggers?" after they hear that she is helping Sofia run Celie's shop, Eleanor Jane has a question of her own: "Who ever heard of somebody like Sofia working for trash" (246). Having heard the whole of Sofia's story from her mother, Eleanor Jane is now in a position to understand that differences need not cancel out mutual respect.

The theme of racial and sexual reconstruction is played out on a large canvas in *The Color Purple*. Nettie's retelling of the African story contains some equally harsh truths, but like the ones told to Albert and Eleanor Jane, hers, too, clear the way for reconciliation. On the racial front, European mythologizing of Africa and its people as backward and mired in poverty is revised to reveal Europe as the cause of the problem it blames the victims for. Not only did Europe rob Africa of priceless art and artifacts that fill up many a museum in the West, but Europe is also responsible for the destruction of African cities and the enslavement of "millions and millions of Africans." The economic rape of Africa continues as European companies push Africans out of the land, destroying their way of life in the process, to make room for rubber and cacao trees, the goods of the marketplace. From this angle, therefore, the philanthropy of such westerners as Doris Baines, who sent two young African girls to England to study medicine and agriculture and "built a hospital, a grammar school [and a] college" in her home town, seems inconsequential (205). In Walker's womanist perspective, however, Doris Baines sketches a picture of hope for the races as she heads for England with her "grandchild" Harold, the son of one of the young women she had helped to educate, by her side. It seems as if Doris has had time to reconsider her earlier colonialist belief that "an African daisy and an English daisy are both flowers but totally different kinds" (127).

Just as Europe's racial myths are challenged in the novel, so are Africa's sexist attitudes held up to public view. The oppressive African mentality, according to Walker, is rooted in self-centeredness, and sexist Africans are as guilty of this crime as are racist (American) whites. "I think Africans are very much like white people back home," Nettie writes, "in that they think they are the center of the universe and that everything that is done is done for them" (155). Through Nettie, Walker, true to her womanist courage, chastises African men for their subjugation of women. So deeply has the belief in male dominance—with female subordination as its corollary—been ingrained in men and women that a mother can say about her girl-child: "A girl is nothing to herself; only to her husband can she become something," which is, of course, "the mother of his children" (144). Thus education is reserved for boys who, when they become men, will care for their wives. The idea of a dependent woman is fixed in the Olinka psyche. "There is always someone to look after Olinka Woman," Tashi's father declares, that "someone" being, of course, a man (149). This sexually oppressive climate replicates the one that nearly stunted Celie's and Nettie's growth under Pa, as Nettie rightly observes: "There is a way that the men speak to women that reminds me too much of Pa. They listen just long enough to issue instructions. They don't even look at women when women are speaking" (149). Those women, such as Tashi's aunt, who fight against this cultural effort to reduce them to ciphers, are sold into slavery, an act that completely effaces their individuality.

Like the system that imprisoned Celie, this canvas of overwhelming masculinity does not escape womanism's brush of change. Young Tashi, reincarnating her aunt's fighting spirit, begins to reveal signs of interiority which are misread in this phallic economy as her slowly "becoming someone else" (148).

Tashi, in fact, molds a personality uniquely her own, and the true test of her liberation comes with her rejection of Adam's marriage proposal because of her fear that in America Adam would want to turn her into someone else—a skimpily dressed, light-skinned (most likely, bleached) woman without a scarred face. Tashi thus sets the terms of marital agreement: she will not trade in her individuality— "the scarification marks on her cheeks" (243) or her black skin, for example—for love. That Adam's reassurance of Tashi goes beyond the promise of eternal fidelity to the scarring of his own face is an indication that relations between women and men have reached a new threshold. Both offshoots of rigidly gendered societies, Tashi and Adam symbolize an emergent sexual consciousness that allows for difference without penalty or privilege.

"Womanist is to feminist as purple is to lavender," Walker writes in *In Search of Our Mothers' Gardens* (xii). Appearing at the end of a list of womanist determinants, this metaphor is intended as a visual illustration of the ideological gap between womanism and feminism. The shade of difference is a matter of depth or intensity. While both modes of thought originate from the same wellspring of resistance to patriarchal domination, womanism intensifies the struggle by fighting from several fronts because it believes that patriarchy, like the Gorgon, is many-headed. More than simply being aware of the "multiple jeopardies of race and class, not the singular one of sexual inequality," the womanist writer is artistically committed to a radical restructuring of society that will allow for the dissolution of boundaries of race, sex and class.[21] What Froula calls "Walker's recreated universe" in *The Color Purple* is a womanist paradigm that offers a rigorous critique of white feminist practices.[22] Complicity in patriarchal thought, the Achilles' heel of the woman writer, is particularly acute in Woolf and Drabble, for example, and the diluted resistance it engenders in their fiction is a blind spot in the white feminist aesthetic that womanism intends to illuminate.

However, while this critique of mainstream feminism rests on legitimate grounds, the *carpe diem* urgency of womanism's dismantle-and-rebuild message seems to overlook Walker's own arduous progress toward her liberatory aesthetic. In other words, Walker's fiction reveals that her feet were held to patriarchal fire long enough for her to be able to appreciate the degree to which the female psyche has been scarred by marginality. The creative imagination of both black and white women has been held captive by the masculine complex (as studies such as Hazel Carby's *Reconstructing Womanhood* and Sandra Gilbert and Susan Gubar's *The Madwoman in the Attic* affirm)[23] and escape routes have often been short-circuited by such other social exigencies as race and class. There is no doubt that Walker has reached a clearing in *The Color Purple*, a space where female subjectivity redefines itself as autonomous and at the same time "as self in relationship."[24] Her creative lens has long pointed in this direction but, as I have demonstrated hers has been an odyssey fraught with doubt, despair, and hope. The picture of Meridian, finally self affirming but totally alienated, that ends that novel stands in sharp contradistinction to the portrait of celebration which rounds off *The Color Purple*.

However, the effort expended toward the achievement of womanism's holistic worldview by no means minimizes its success. The womanist perspective is an important contribution to the feminist project. As Linda Alcoff puts it, "You cannot mobilize a movement that is only and always against: you must have a positive alternative, a vision of a better future that can motivate people to sacrifice their time and energy toward its realization."[25] That the womanist goal holds such a vision is indisputable. What is problematic is the essentialist implication of womanism's self-definition. A womanist as "black feminist" or "feminist of color" not only excludes white feminists whose creative vision approximates the womanist ideal (Agnes Smedley, for example) or those who might choose to incorporate aspects of womanism in their writing, especially in the wake of the recent push for inclusiveness in feminist theory. It also assumes that by virtue of being black or nonwhite, a feminist is necessarily womanist. The example of Buchi Emecheta, which is the subject of the next chapter, seems to complicate Walker's effort to racially limit the womanist ethic.

4

The Joys of Motherhood

A STUDY OF A PROBLEMATIC
WOMANIST AESTHETIC

We have seen how the married woman and the widowed woman
and even the divorced woman are defined by their relationship to
men, a father or a husband or their sons . . . women have been
driven to this position where they may only live through men. So
great is the power of tradition that no single woman in Africa, in
spite of her awareness, is able to shift the power of tradition.

Lauretta Ngcobo, "African Motherhood—Myth and Reality"

In 1976 when Alice Walker in a review of *Second Class Citizen*
praised Buchi Emecheta for her ability to write fiction amidst
the turbulence of child care, she probably was not aware that
she had more in common with this budding writer and mother
than the same birth year (1944) and the desire for imaginative
(over and above physical) fecundity.[1] Indebted to an oral tradition, both writers were not only inspired by female *griottes*
—Walker's mother and Emecheta's "big mother" or aunt—
but also some of their stories are actually renditions of the
tales that had fed their childhood imagination. Both writers
also experienced the near destruction of their creative inheritance by racial bigotry. In college, Walker's expression of her
wish to become a poet was met by "a white Northerner['s]"
suggestion "that a 'farmer's daughter' might not be the stuff
of which poets are made" (*Gardens* 18). Miss Humble, one of
Emecheta's teachers in her Methodist high school, was just as

crudely incredulous in her reaction to young Buchi's declaration of her desire to be a writer. Cloaking her racism in the
all-too-familiar Christian admonition against pride, she ordered Emecheta to the chapel to pray "for God's forgiveness."[2]
That both writers should choose to harken to the voices of
their female kin (to think back through their mothers, as
Woolf would say) and defy the authority of their detractors
points to a shared sense of purpose and determination.

Walker's delineation of womanism should forge yet another
link between herself and Emecheta. Being "black" and "feminist," Emecheta satisfies two important womanist criteria
and by broaching the once mute subject of African male dominance and its corollary, female subordination, she clearly
partakes of the "audacious" spirit Walker ascribes to the
womanist writer. Lloyd Brown, one of the first critics of African women's writing, describes Emecheta as "the most sus-
tained and vigorous voice of direct, feminist protest" and sees
her as almost unique in her "intensity and directness when
describing sexual inequality and female dependence."[3] However, though Emecheta deserves credit for the "womanish"
spirit underlying her engagement with African patriarchal
society, she does not fit easily into the womanist slot as Walker
defines it in *The Color Purple*. Pressed to the service of the
woman-centered yet sexually and racially integrated world of
womanism, Emecheta's fiction breaks down under the burden
of authorial ambiguity. Sexual and racial messages are mixed
as Emecheta oscillates between rebellion and submission.

It is the kind of self-division feminist analysis has iden-
tified as the inevitable consequence of women's creative effort
within the dominant androcentric culture the kind evident in
the fiction of Woolf and Drabble. In Emecheta, the problem
is exacerbated by the competing demands of two opposing
cultures—African and Western. Uncompromising in her ex-
posure of the cultural confinement of African women, Emecheta is nonetheless reluctant to engage large social issues,
partly because, as she admits, "I don't deal with great ideological issues. I write about the little happenings of everyday

life."[4] Emecheta, like many African women writers, also tries to avoid the ideological snare Ngũgĩ wa Thiong'o calls a "cultural bomb," that imperialist tool used "to annihilate a people's belief in their names, in their languages, in their environment, in their heritage of struggle, in their unity, in their capacities and ultimately in themselves." This weapon, wa Thiong'o argues, is as effective in the hands of Africa's "neo-colonial bourgeoisie" as it has been in the colonizer's hands.[5] The nationalistic implications of wa Thiong'o's statement constitute a dilemma for African feminist writers who believe that existing forms of nationalism in Africa serve the interest of patriarchy. Aware of the necessary conflict between feminism and a narrowly conceived nationalism, many of these writers have difficulty engaging simultaneously female subordination and existing nationalist concerns.[6] In Emecheta's case, life in England gave her a new perspective of the west in relation to Africa. Her experience with the brutal reality of London life expunged from her mind the colonial myths of Europe's moral supremacy. As she put it in an interview, "Many Nigerians, who came in contact with missionaries or British officials, thought on the basis of that experience that all whites were pure of heart and pleasant in character," a notion that "often went up in smoke" when they got to Britain.[7] In her autobiography Emecheta paints a chilling portrait of the English spirit: "England gave me a cold welcome. As I said in *Second Class Citizen*, 'If I had been Jesus, I would have passed England by and not dropped a single blessing.' It felt like walking into the inside of a grave."[8] The Empire thus strikes back, an interesting coda to the racial and cultural narrative inscribed in *Mrs. Dalloway.*

Loyalty and resistance characterize Emecheta's fictional voice—the former stemming from her rootedness in African culture and the latter from her opposition to women's place within it. Seeking a way out of this dilemma, she advances an individualistic concept of female emancipation that resonates more with the feminist strategies of Woolf and Drabble than with Walker's womanist tactics. Though she lacks Drabble's decidedly fatalistic vision of female possibility and certainly Woolf's privileging of an ungendered aesthetics, Emecheta nonetheless shares their over-determined view of masculinity, an attitude womanism sets out to explode and reconstitute. As the site of undiminished male authority, thwarted female possibility, and demarcated racial realities, Emecheta's fiction eschews the womanist project of challenge and change, a fact that is most powerfully dramatized in her fifth novel, *The Joys of Motherhood*. Before turning to the problematics of womanism in this novel, I will first examine those features of feminism found in Emecheta's earlier works that crystallize into an unwomanist praxis.

In keeping with their autobiographical tenor, the first two novels, *In the Ditch* and *Second Class Citizen*, posit a personal ethos as resolution to the problem of female oppression: individual women, like Adah, Emecheta's alter ego, can be weavers of their own destiny. In an implacably oppressive masculine society, woman is thrown back on herself to effect her own rescue. It is she, not the system that oppresses her, who must change from a creature trapped in dependency to an adult set free by education and economic self-sufficiency. In effect, Emecheta offers her own story of success in the face of insurmountable odds as paradigm for female liberation. If Adah, embodying as she does the ultimate sexual and racial Other, can claw her way out of the hardened racism of London society, her Nigerian husband's ingrained sexism, and grinding poverty, the self-willed woman can thus by inference defy and defeat the forces of her oppression. In both *In The Ditch*, which Chikwenye Ogunyemi aptly describes as "an extended praise poem of Adah in her struggle to survive without a husband, tied down by five children, in a hostile environment," and in *Second Class Citizen*, Adah's "second-class status of being African, female and poor is counter balanced by [her] 'first-class' capacity for independence and creativity."[9] Thus Emecheta sets up the indefatigable Adah as a paragon of female indomitability.

This strategy has serious drawbacks, artistically and ideologically. First of all, the novels' underlying assumption that the strong-willed woman can achieve selfhood clashes violently with the unrelenting current of protest directed at a system that is determined to keep Adah "in the ditch" and "a second-class citizen." It seems Emecheta wants to dismantle patriarchy only to make room for her model female rather than to expose its self-privileging arrangements. For example, responding to Francis's refusal to treat her as his equal during a domestic emergency, Adah sets herself apart from the run of womankind she, in effect, deems deserving of male slight:

> Adah could no longer bear the suspense. She was impatient, and was beginning to hate it all. She hated being treated like a *native woman* who was not supposed to know the important happenings in her family until they had been well discussed and analyzed by the menfolk.[10]

Whether one reads "native" as "simple" or "unsophisticated" (which is, most likely, Emecheta's primary meaning) or as denoting essence (that is, "natural" woman), Adah's self-representation as unique and different from the female species is the final impression. A self-will that brooks no masculine prerogative is Adah's trademark and, in Emecheta's view, compelling grounds for her admission into the world of "menfolk" (69). In Walker's womanist universe, self-willed women like Shug Avery are saboteurs of patriarchy and, more crucially, situate themselves within a female collective.

Adah is also psychologically suited for battle with London's racist patriarchy. While her fellow transplanted Ibos (including her husband) stoically bear the burden of their second-class status, Adah deploys a strategy that does not lose sight of her eventual goal of equality with England's first-class citizenry: she will not succumb to the view that she is inferior because she is black. An unmitigated pragmatist, however, Adah will play at being subaltern while she searches for an escape route into the mainstream, but her self-identity will remain intact:

> This is where she differed from Francis and the others. They believed that one had to start with the inferior and

stay there, because being black meant being inferior . . . she started to act in the way expected of her because she was still new in England, but after a while she was not going to accept it from anyone. She was going to regard herself as the equal of any white. (P. 71)

By hypostatizing Adah, Emecheta invalidates her own voice of protest. If it has been textually predetermined that Adah should both beat and join the system, one wonders why Emecheta should rail against that system, except perhaps to underscore her heroine's preternatural strength of will. This artistic incongruity results in (or, perhaps, stems from) what Lloyd Brown calls an "ideological fuzziness or a certain degree of naivete" that characterizes Emecheta's novels in general but is particularly evident in the first two.[11] Doubly marginalized as female and colonial subject, Emecheta gravitates toward a male center of subjectivity under the unexamined assumption that the black woman can overcome the barriers of race and sex through confidence in her capacity to survive.

This model of black womanhood, drawing on the stereotype of the strong, resilient black woman that Joyce Ladner cautions us against in *Tomorrow's Tomorrow*, may have left Emecheta in a tight ideological spot, given her understanding of the African woman's condition and her inclination to protest it. Adah, in all her remarkable resourcefulness, is matchless, and her anomalous success story overlooks the reality of the African woman as an object of male transaction who, to borrow Shoshana Felman's apt description of the female predicament, "is first and foremost a daughter/a mother/a wife."[12] And so the optimism of the first two books gives way to the stark realism of the next three— *The Bride Price, The Slave Girl,* and *The Joys of Motherhood*—as Emecheta explores the barely traveled terrain of African femininity and uncovers the chilling facts about the social victimization of African women. This paradigm-shift from woman as exemplar to woman as victim, however, is accompanied by the same ideological ambivalence evidenced in the earlier novels: resistance against male authority is undermined by deference to it.

The Bride Price, Emecheta's third novel, ushers in a world that is distant from the busy traffic of London depicted in the preceding books but very close to Emecheta because it is the world of her childhood and early adulthood. The novelist imaginatively returns home to Nigeria to trace the roots of her own thinking (and Adah's) about the sexes, and what she unearths is a belief deeply embedded in the cultural psyche of female secondariness. Aku-nna, Emecheta's heroine, spends her growing years learning the cultural script that inscribes women as objects of exchange among men and sources for male pleasure. Aku-nna reads in the custom that transfers her mother to her dead husband's brother, for example, the fate that awaits her. Her mother's desperate longing for another boy child also informs Aku-nna of woman's secondary place in the human hierarchy, a fact Aku-nna's uncle's growing interest in her bride price (her monetary value) confirms.

Determined not to be a victim, like her mother, of gender injustice, Aku-nna commits a double transgression: she marries a man of her own choosing and ignores the sanction that, by his slave ancestry, makes him a social outcast. By linking Aku-nna and Chike, Emecheta conflates the roles of woman and slave, setting in motion the woman-as-slave metaphor that pervades her fiction. It is clear, too, that the author applauds the lovers' magnificent rebellion against the social proscription that desiccates their lives, as she leads them through a terrain of oppressive customs (including Aku-nna's kidnapping and near-rape) into a state of matrimonial bliss. But their happiness is short-lived. With her bride-price unpaid (because her uncle refuses to negotiate with Chike's family of slaves), Aku-nna dies at the end of the novel to propitiate the gods of custom. Patriarchal law is thus rendered ineluctable and the novel's womanist promise expires alongside Aku-nna's childbirth-ravaged body. Emecheta's rupture of womanist expectations in this and other novels is a sign of her cultural ambivalence: opposition that belies allegiance to Africa's traditions. As if rethinking Adah's successful defiance in *In the Ditch* and *Second Class Citizen,* Emecheta offers *The Bride Price* as a cautionary tale for would-be rebels:

So it was that Chike and Aku-nna substantiated the traditional superstition they had unknowingly set out to eradicate. Every girl born after Aku-nna's death was told her
story, to reinforce the old taboos of the land. If a girl wished
to live long and see her children's children, she must accept
the husband chosen for her by her people, and the bride
price must be paid. If the bride price was not paid, she
would never survive the birth of her first child.[13]

In an interview, the author not only confirms the novel's
concession to tradition but also implicates herself directly in
Aku-nna's demise and its inevitability:

The social and mental pressure is so great that I let her die.
She had to die because she broke with tradition. . . . I,
too, am ashamed that my bride price was not paid. Maybe
my marriage failed because of that. You see how deep certain traditions fasten themselves to your spirit. You have
the feeling of being an outcast, cut off from your own
background.[14]

Thus Aku-nna is both scapegoat and victim and her death
appeases her creator's conscience as much as it satisfies the
guardians of tradition. That Emecheta should find it necessary to fictionally atone for her own "crime" against culture
is an indication of the strength of cultural traditions and their
effect on the creative mind.

In *The Slave Girl*, Emecheta once more stalks patriarchy
long enough to evoke the specter of womanhood incarnated
in otherness. The novel is a bildungsroman that maps out the
trajectory of a young woman's psychological development
from forced slavery to self-imposed vassalage. Ojebeta, Emecheta's orphaned heroine, is sold into slavery at the tender age
of seven by a rapacious brother for the measly sum of eight
pounds, money he claims he needs to buy a dance outfit for
the ritual marking his passage into manhood.[15] Female selfhood is thus regarded as essentially irrelevant. Emecheta's
disapproval of this act of violation is powerfully evident in
her portrayal of its perpetrator, Okolie, Ojebeta's shameless
betrayer:

He did not want to work hard at farming, as most members
of his age-group did to raise money for their outing prepa-
rations: not only would that take a long time but the work
was too strenuous. Had not his late father always called
him a good-for-nothing . . . fit only to go about blowing
horn-pipes for funeral ceremonies or at bride departures?
. . . Some small children had already started calling him
"Okolie Ujo Ugbo"—Okolie the farm truant—for when
other young men were out on their farms during the day he
was seen walking about doing nothing. (Pp. 40–41)

Like the father of Achebe's hero in *Things Fall Apart*, Okolie
as individual man is a failure. But as social man and benefi-
ciary of what Catherine Stimpson calls "the triumph of the
wilful masculine over the feminine," he is empowered with
absolute authority over his sister's being.[16] Though he feels a
tinge of conscience and worries about the moral judgment of
others, Okolie is as certain about the rightness of his act as
Emecheta is about its wrongness. But as her tone of disapproval gives way to an unhurried portrait of the enslaved
(Ojebeta and her fellow thralls) making a virtue of necessity,
Emecheta is once more backing out of confrontation with
culture and placing the burden of change on women rather
than on society. Chameleon-like, Ojebeta, like Adah before
her, adapts to an oppressive environment by cultivating the
author's favorite virtue: an unbent will. As proof of her ac-
climatization, the novel ends with the easy transfer of Ojebeta
from the restrictive confines of Ma Palagada's slave colony
into the entrapment of marriage:

So as Britain was emerging from war once more victorious,
claiming to have stopped the slavery which she had helped
to spread in all her black colonies, Ojebeta, now a woman
of thirty-five, was changing masters. (P. 179)

Wedding the heroine's predicament and Britain's patriarchal and colonial habits seems every bit womanist, but,
given the mere tweaking of the system that occurs in the rest
of the novel, Emecheta's last-minute knockout punch is more
autotelic than womanist. After the initial shock of sibling be-

trayal when Okolie palms his sister off for a few pounds, the novel crests on the benevolent portrait of slavery, showing Ojebeta gaining rather than losing respectability. And when we see her for the last time, she is oozing gratitude because Jacob, her husband, has repurchased her by paying her bride price and has thus "rightly valued" her. The heavy satirical note on which Emecheta ends, therefore, is not held up by the general mood of the novel, which, though critical of female social disadvantage, is mindful of male authority in an un-womanist way.

The most obvious example of the difficulty attending Eme-cheta's attempt to recuperate womanhood occurs in *The Joys of Motherhood.* Ironically, this novel is the ripest with oppor-tunity for challenge, and Emecheta comes close to throwing down the gauntlet. But, as the title suggests, it is the wisdom of irony that prevails as the author backs out of a potentially womanist confrontation with an entrenched system of male dominance. The joylessness of the much-touted happy insti-tution of motherhood is thus the trope that is intended to carry the author's message of woman's predicament. Unfor-tunately, women are caught by social forces larger than any metaphoric trapdoor, and while Emecheta succeeds in cap-turing their menacing presence, she fails to provide any pos-sibility of rescue from them. Here, too, as in *The Bride Price,* the cult of masculinity proves implacable and once more woman is the sacrificial offering.

The novel presents two orders of being: male and female, with the male state as primary and self-delineating and the female, subordinate and trapped in the prison-house of the "second sex." In this sexual economy, women serve men as wives, daughters, and mothers, and each role exacts total sub-mission and self-abnegation. The opening chapter functions as a caveat, the discrepancy between the benign title and the wrenching episode it announces alerting the reader to the complications that underlie social categories. Nnu Ego, the heroine, is seen one morning on a Lagos street in a mad rush to end her life. Emecheta's narrative strategy is not to spell out the reason behind Nnu Ego's suicidal urge but to provide sufficient hints for readers to make an educated guess. Nnu Ego, we are told, feels "pain in her young and unsupported breasts, now filling fast with milk since the birth of her baby boy four weeks before." Her mind too is filled—with thoughts of "her baby . . . her baby!" When she "involuntarily" grabs her breasts, it is "more for assurance of her motherhood than to ease their weight."[17] Finally Nnu Ego wonders why "her *chi*, her personal god . . . had punished her so" (9). The picture, then, is of a young woman driven to the edge by the loss of her newly born son. We are, indeed, entering a world where, in Adrienne Rich's words, "female possibility has been literally massacred on the site of motherhood," a world all too familiar to many Drabblean heroines.[18]

For Nnu Ego, the massacre includes not just her "possibility," but her life. Hers is the harrowing tale of a woman crushed to death by the physical and emotional weight of the institution of motherhood. Humiliated and rejected by her first husband because she could not have a child, Nnu Ego is passed on by her father to another man whom she despises so deeply at their first encounter that she thinks of returning home. As despicable as Nnaife is, however, Nnu Ego sees him as the man who could save her from the stigma of barrenness, a fate worse than death. Her wish becomes reality and indeed, the fact that "this child was a son gave her a sense of fulfillment for the first time in her life" (54). Her happiness is short-lived, however. Nnu Ego's son dies and she opts for death rather than life as "a failed woman" (62). After her suicide attempt is aborted, she settles into a life of unabated childbearing that leaves her physically and emotionally spent. Nine childbirths later, with seven surviving children, Nnu Ego returns to her father's village to die, a broken woman, deserted by all her children but in particular by the sons she had prayed so hard and worried so long to have for her husband. Nnu Ego's tragedy is rooted in the cultural imperative of Ibo society as much as in her creator's ideological ambivalence.

Emecheta has received considerable praise for her feminist consciousness. Marie Umeh, for example, sees her as an "artist preoccupied with change . . . an iconoclast [who in *The Joys of Motherhood*] breaks away from the prevalent portraitures in African writing in which motherhood is honorific."[19] For Katherine Frank, "Emecheta's account of African womanhood is the unapologetically feminist one."[20] And Eustace Palmer, linking Achebe and Emecheta in their evocation of traditional African society, points to the latter's "disgust at male chauvinism" and dissatisfaction with "an unfair and oppressive system."[21] The case for Emecheta's radical feminism may well be overstated, given the dialectic of repudiation and identification that characterizes her fiction.

Feminist critical discourse on the politics of subversion sheds important light on Emecheta's textual practice. Many critics view the phenomenon of self-division in the woman writer as proof of women's ability to negotiate a space for themselves within patriarchal discourse. Catherine Stimpson, for example, sees Gertrude Stein as so adept at doubling that she "dislodges our trust even in her residually patriarchal messages about gender."[22] Deirdre David is fascinated by "the resistance to and the complicity with hegemonic patriarchy" of three Victorian female luminaries—Harriet Martineau, Elizabeth Barrett Browning, and George Eliot—although she does not let her women off the patriarchal hook so easily as Stimpson does Stein.[23] And Marianne DeKoven, citing as examples Kate Chopin's *The Awakening* and Charlotte Perkins Gilman's *The Yellow Wallpaper*, locates modern women writers' "endemic ambivalence" within "the inherent doubleness of modernist form," a context she deems beneficial rather than harmful to "the expression of feminist content."[24]

If, as I argue in chapter 3, the womanist achievement of *The Color Purple* is the displacement of ambivalence as a necessary tool for female response to patriarchy, then Emecheta's strategy of resistance and accommodation in *The Joys of Motherhood* should be characterized as feminist rather than womanist, in spite of Walker's race-specific definition of womanism.

Indeed, when DeKoven labels the "textual structure" of *The Awakening* an "oscillation between assertion and retreat" (26), she could easily be speaking of Emecheta's novel. *The Joys of Motherhood* is replete with duality that I believe, unlike those who sympathize with feminist ambivalence, is ultimately self-defeating. One glowing example involves the credibility of the heroine as a passive character. Nnu Ego is the love-child of two proud, self-centered individuals of legendary fame. Her father's haughty and domineering manner was befitting a man who, as a "wealthy local chief," was also titled (10). In her mother, however, assertiveness and vanity met with societal rebuke; Ona, "priceless jewel" (11) that she was, was determined to live out the full significance of her name by refusing to be wedded to Agbadi, who would own her for always once he paid her bride price. And so as Ona teased, taunted, and romanced the man she loved, she proudly wore her badge of dishonor as "a bad woman," that is, one "who was troublesome and impetuous, who had the audacity to fight with her man before letting him have her" (21). Some good did come out of Ona's bad reputation, however: she signified a vital female self-presence that would brook no contingency. Long after her death Ona would be remembered as a different breed of woman, one who refused to concede male superiority.

Aware of the implications of placing a self-creating woman in a decidedly masculine society, Emecheta moves swiftly to obliterate Ona. In two brief, ambiguous sentences, Ona and her rebellious spirit are laid to rest: "After the birth, Ona was weak but her head was clear. She knew she was dying" (28). Ona dies not just literally but figuratively, too. In time she is safely removed to the realm of myth, as Idayi fondly reminisces sixteen years later that "they don't make women like her any more" (30). And Emecheta does not allow traces of Ona's aberrant behavior to survive in her daughter. While Ona was a smasher of custom's idols, Nnu Ego is a faithful worshipper at their altar; there, as if in atonement for her mother's act of sacrilege, she ends up ultimately as the most appeasing sacrifice. That Nnu Ego, the issue of two persons whose combined characters spell superciliousness, should turn out to be the embodiment of docility may strike us as illogical but Emecheta seems more interested in her heroine's suitability to an idea of African womanhood than in breaking the chains which the culture has forged.

While Emecheta seems to highlight her heroine's self-denying traits, careful reading reveals evidence of a strong self-protective streak in Nnu Ego which the author narratively short-circuits. A telling example is the scene where Nnu Ego lashes at her co-wife's female visitor because she feels almost naked in the presence of the regally dressed woman. Though the effectiveness of the scene as a barometer of Nnu Ego's character is nearly destroyed by over-dramatization, it nonetheless provides convincing evidence of her impulse for self-interest. The woman's opulence, mockingly mirroring Nnu Ego's own state of destitution, opens up a floodgate of envy:

> *And look at her,* Nnu Ego thought angrily, *look at the expensive shoes she is wearing, look at that headtie, and even a gold chain—all this just to come and see her relative Adaku, and in this rain! God, the cost of that headtie! Whatever she paid for it would feed me and the children for a whole month. And she is the daughter of a nobody! Yet look at me, the daughter of a well-known chief, reduced to this.* (P. 163)

The anger expressed here at thwarted possibility, however, swiftly dissipates before it does any serious damage to Nnu Ego's outward image of self-renunciation. Silence and solicitude divert the strong current of feeling inside so that not even ripples are visible. As Nnu Ego reverts to her role as senior wife, a position that requires her to abandon her personality in order to affirm her husband's, she looks more like one who is sinned against (by her creator) than one who sins.

Nnu's generally repressed tendency toward self-expression also surfaces in her dealings with Adaku, her husband's second wife. As Nnu Ego's foil, Adaku refracts her rival's shortcomings because her rejection of societal validation stands in stark contrast to Nnu Ego's ceaseless quest for approbation. Adaku also acts as a bait, however, drawing out into the open Nnu Ego's hidden self, which is in fact desire-ridden and in conflict with her sacrificial public mien. For instance, after Nnaife loses his washerman's job with the Meers family, Nnu Ego is forced into penny-pinching habits which are as exacting as her incontinent husband. Nonetheless she endures the strain in relative silence, as she empties herself into chores, occasionally prodding her husband to seek reemployment. With Adaku's arrival, however, Nnu Ego's pent-up desire for better circumstances explodes, first because of resentment over opportunities lost:

> Nnu Ego felt that she should be bowing to this perfect creature—she who had once been acclaimed the most beautiful woman ever seen. What had happened to her? Why had she become so haggard, so worn, when this one looked like a pool that had still to be disturbed? (P. 118)

Second, Nnu Ego fears encroachment on her life, even as spare and unenviable as it is: "She was used to being the sole woman of this house, used to having Nnaife all to herself, planning with him what to do with the little money he earned. . . . But now this new menace" (118).

If we combine this spontaneous display of self-concern with Nnu Ego's ill-concealed envy of Adaku's well-being and of her work ethic, the picture belies the image of one who lacks all focus on herself. The fact is, desire—both material and sexual—ferments in Nnu Ego as much as it did in the success-driven heroine of the first two novels. But whereas in Adah, whose life and ideology more closely resemble Emecheta's own, that yearning was allowed to effervesce, in Nnu Ego it fizzles out under the weight of an outward conduct of self-rejection. Sexual desire constitutes a significant aspect of Nnu Ego's being. On the night of Adaku's noisy lovemaking with Nnaife, Nnu Ego actively participates in the scene's eroticism. Enacting in her imagination the physical act taking place a curtain away from her, Nnu Ego "bites her teeth

into her baby's night clothes to prevent herself from scream-
ing" (125), an action that is clearly orgasmic. But true to the
duplicity that rules her identity, Nnu Ego tries to repress even
these feelings by defining them as inappropriate in marriage.

The consequence of thwarted desire is madness, defined by
Shoshana Felman as "the impasse confronting those whom
cultural conditioning has deprived of the very means of protest and self-affirmation."[25] Forced to vitiate her female self in
order to affirm and perpetuate, as breeder of men, male existence, Nnu Ego seeks solace in the healing numbness that
insanity provides. It is not a coincidence that in the two instances of full-blown madness—the suicide attempt which
opens the novel and the state of dissolution which ends it—
death is within a hair's-breadth of madness. For Nnu Ego,
both are routes of escape, far more reliable than the lame, last-
minute option of wakeful consciousness offered by her creator.

Nnu Ego's sudden awakening to the reality of women's
and her own oppression is a *deus ex machina* that is problematic, and comparing it to Celie's coming to consciousness
in *The Color Purple* draws attention to the opposing ideological
agendas of Walker and Emecheta. As the noblest incarnation
of her culture's ideals, Nnu Ego is not a reliable instrument of
change. Hers is no longer a *tabula rasa* which, like Celie's, is
awaiting inscription. Rather, it has been fully and faithfully
inscribed with cultural dicta that she wholeheartedly endorses.
As a favorite child, she learned well at her father's knee the
important lesson that society's expectations must be met, not
questioned. Her first marriage serves as a test case, as Nnu
Ego dutifully absorbs the emotional abuse heaped on her because of her alleged barrenness. Rather than find fault with
Amatokwu's overweening masculinity, Nnu Ego instead
blames and punishes herself for failing her husband, in ac-
cordance with the mandates of the cultural script. Moreover,
despite Amatokwu's shabby behavior he represents for Nnu
Ego a masculine ideal which she recalls longingly whenever
Nnaife, her second husband, reveals one of his many shortcomings. Neither the triple burdens she carries as daughter,
wife, and mother nor the liberating example of the self-willed

Adaku has the force to cut Nnu Ego loose from the cultural moorings that secure her to female secondariness.

It is surprising, therefore, that after a life of constraint and submission, punctuated by infrequent instances of mild resistance, Nnu Ego should finally find a voice of her own:

> "God, when will you create a woman who will be fulfilled in herself, a full human being, not anybody's appendage?" she prayed desperately. "After all, I was born alone, and I shall die alone. What have I gained from all this? Yes, I have many children, but what do I have to feed them on? On my life, I have to work myself to the bone to look after them. I have to give them my all. . . . When will I be free?" (Pp. 186–87)

The answer to that rhetorical question is self-evident but Nnu Ego provides it anyway:

> Never, not even in death. I am a prisoner of my own flesh and blood. Is it such an enviable position? The men make it look as if we must aspire for children or die. That's why when I lost my first son I wanted to die, because I failed to live up to the standard expected of me by the males in my life, my father and my husband—and now I have to include my sons. But who made the law that we should not hope in our daughters? We women subscribe to that law more than anyone. Until we change all this, it is still a man's world, which we women will always help to build. (P. 187)

So incongruous is this complaint/confession with the heroine's psychological portrait that one is inclined to suspect a voice-over rather than Nnu Ego's own voice. Emecheta could easily be chafing against the brutal restrictions imposed on women about which, it seems, she can only equivocate. This momentary outpouring of anger and guilt seems to project the author's dilemma more than it reflects a reappraisal by Nnu Ego who, with quiet, elemental dignity, continues on the path of self-destruction. Authorial intrusion is a notable characteristic of Emecheta's narrative style. Commentary that injects the narrator into the plot is not uncommon in her novels. For example, responding to the communal effort to block Nnu Ego's suicide attempt, the narrator observes that

> a thing like that is not permitted in Nigeria, you are simply not allowed to commit suicide in peace, because everyone is responsible for the other person. Foreigners may call *us* a nation of busybodies, but to *us*, an individual's life belongs to the community and not just to him or her. (P. 60; emphasis added)

The first-person plural pronoun signals Emecheta's intention not to be a detached recorder of events but rather to partake of the emotional investment of her tale—that is, until the ground shifts to sexual politics. Here, Emecheta balks because, according to her view of women's place in traditional African societies, the stakes are too high. Consider Emecheta's recollection of her own mother, who suffered silently under an oppressive patriarchal system and "who probably loved me in her own way, but never expressed it; my mother, that slave girl who had the courage to free herself and return to her people in Ibusa, and still stooped and allowed the culture of her people to re-enslave her."[26] As daughter and writer Emecheta seeks to break her mother's silence but she too recognizes the consequences of female speech. Hence Nnu Ego serves Emecheta as a safe mouthpiece for voicing frustration over her double silencing as woman and writer, without what Marianne DeKoven calls "fear of punishment for female anger and desire."[27] Registered through her entropic heroine, however, protest is leveled to mere words and inaction, and male power persists unperturbed.

What distinguishes Celie's awakening from Nnu Ego's is her refusal to reinstate masculine authority once she has "wised up" to its fictions. Nnu Ego's cry for freedom is not a challenge; rather it is a complaint, a lament over unrequited affection. Having given her "all" to men and received nothing in return, she is expected to fold up and die—as indeed she does. Yet as shattering as this recognition of her insignificance is, it fails to trigger in Nnu Ego any unbelief in male superiority. Indeed, after admitting to women's and her own complicity in a sexual economy that short-changes women, she is back in business, this time reinvesting in her sons for a worry-free future.

Celie's entry into consciousness, on the contrary, is a revolutionary act that launches a new sexual (and human) order. The challenge thrown at Albert—that until he acknowledges, repents, and corrects the evil he perpetrated against Celie, he is a doomed man—forecloses any possibility of extending male rule. Instead, it clears the way for a new dispensation. Behind Celie's ultimatum lies the moral authority of a writer who, in this novel, will settle for nothing short of a complete overhaul of the existing social system. At the end of her novel, Emecheta seeks the aid of irony once more in a last-ditch effort to empower her heroine. In death, Nnu Ego is finally able to act: she rejects worried women's pleas for fertility. This other-worldly *coup d'etat*, a strategy that recalls Mrs. Ramsay's dominion in death in *To the Lighthouse*, has no place in *The Color Purple*, where the elevation of women in a restructured, material world is the primary goal.

The Joys of Motherhood cannot be said to contribute to the womanist idea of whole(some)ness. Just as the sexes remain divided, the races are ensconced in a superior/inferior binary that is disturbed only slightly by the overseas marriage between Oshia and "a white woman" (224). This interracial marriage, however, is merely a news item tagged on at the end of the novel to suggest the possibility of change in the lives of the future generation. Meanwhile, the colonial attitude regarding the races organizes itself throughout the text along strict master/servant lines. England's imperialistic economy, captured in *Mrs. Dalloway*, is embodied in the racial and class differences between the Meers family and their servants. Like Woolf, Emecheta exposes the colonizing mentality and its effect on the colonized. The custodians of Empire—Dr. and Mrs. Meers—are equipped with prevailing stereotypes of African men that run the gamut from beasts to boys. Their cultivated distance from their domestic help, which includes a disdain for African names, confirms their faith in the ideology of racial difference that gripped the European imagination in the nineteenth century. Dr. Meers's reference to Nnaife as "baboon," (41) to his servants' residence as "boys' quarters" (63), and Mrs. Meers's "meaningless smile" (84), all intone the well-practiced grammar of nineteenth-century racialism.[28]

Interestingly, it is Mrs. Meers who bears the brunt of Emecheta's colonial critique. The "comparatively young woman" with the "grey . . . sunken . . . eyes of a cat" has "an aged look" that seems almost sinister (83–84). While neither she nor her husband rise above their role as stock characters, Dr. Meers remains safely barricaded behind the image of "white master" (41) while his wife suffers the indignity of talking to the servants and of being talked about by them. Nnaife's washing of Mrs. Meers's underwear and Nnu Ego's resentment of that fact combine to dehumanize the colonial woman.

Emecheta throws a few critical jabs at the colonized as well. For example, Nnaife's contentment in double servitude —as washerman and colonial subject—is conveyed with comic irony:

> His heart began to beat fast. He decided to start whistling so that the Madam would not guess that he was aware of her approach. When he saw her, he pulled himself up straighter, his sagging stomach nicely tucked into khaki shorts, and ironed his washing with such a flourish one might have believed the whole world belonged to him. Mrs. Meers stood there by the door. . . . She did not speak, but listened to the noisily cheerful and unconcerned way Nnaife whistled "Abide With Me," as if the tune was one of his native victory songs. (P. 83)

This picture of pathetic obsequiousness is one of a few clear markers of the author's political ideology. But, on the whole, Emecheta seems reluctant to engage the subject of racial politics, in keeping, perhaps, with her avowed intent to eschew "great ideological issues" in her writing.[29] Authorial commentary even deracializes Dr. Meers's unabashedly racist "Goodnight, baboon" remark to Nnaife:

Nnaife did not realise that Dr. Meers's laughter was inspired by that type of wickedness that reduces any man,
white or black, intelligent or not, to a new low; lower than
the basest of animals for animals at least respected each
other's feelings, each other's dignity. (P. 42)

For a moment, the passage's animal imagery invites the suspicion that Emecheta might actually be about to even the
score with Dr. Meers, but the generic "any man" and the racially neutral "white or black" soon frustrate that line of
thinking. Attention is further diverted from the racial insult
by Nnaife's sexist observation that "Women were all the same"
as he listens to Mrs. Meers shower her husband with a torrent
of words during a spat (42). Thus as a victim of racism who,
in turn, victimizes women, Nnaife loses the reader's sympathy
and Emecheta backs out of a tight racial spot.

The racial rapprochement achieved in *The Color Purple* is
apt to elude Emecheta and other African women writers in
the face of existing nationalist ideologies. The movement to
decolonize the African mind encompasses a range of strategies of which the most salient are aimed at literary production. Ngũgĩ wa Thiong'o, the Kenyan writer, presents the
case in terms of "Uhuru wa Bendera" (freedom of the flag)
versus psychic freedom. In a 1972 conference held in Nairobi
to map the contours of a postcolonial African literary discourse, wa Thiong'o warned his audience against the lure of
"the white liberal's dream of a day when black and white can
love one another without going through the agony of violent
reckoning," for liberalism, he affirmed, is nothing more than
"sugary . . . imperialism: it fosters the illusion in the ex-
ploited of the possibilities of peaceful settlement." Defining
literature as an instrument of "cultural struggle and cultural
assertion," wa Thiong'o reminded his audience of the imperatives that inaugurated the African literary project: "the
very act of writing was itself a testimony of the creative capacity of the African and the first tottering but still important
steps by the 'educated' elite toward self-definition and the ac-
ceptance of the environment from which they had been alienated by western, Eurocentric imperialist education."[30]

The call to reinscribe Africanness in African literature has culminated in wa Thiongo's repudiation of English and the establishment of his native Kenyan language of Gĩkũyũ as the appropriate vehicle of his own creative imagination. Bidding farewell to English in 1977 after his fourth novel, *Petals of Blood*, wa Thiong'o has since spearheaded the crusade against what he calls "cultural imperialism," the main targets being the educated "native elite" whose not-yet-deprogrammed minds, he fears, could "help prop up the [British] Empire."[31] To avert this threat, the authors of *Toward the Decolonization of African Literature* posit "an active nationalist consciousness" that would foster a climate of cultural cohesiveness.[32]

This is the intellectual soil in which women writers in contemporary Africa have been trying over the past three decades to establish roots. Resisting women's marginalization within the male-defined nationalist discourses, they simultaneously fear cultural deracination, because African female identity is grounded as much in nation, culture, and race as in gender. Attempts to reframe the debate on nation have generally been regarded as a provocation with potentially dire nationalistic consequences. As Nigerian poet and critic Molara Ogundipe-Leslie puts it, the African woman writer is "usually seen as the cause of whatever happens negatively in the country. The national scapegoat. The cause of the nation's decline."[33] The resultant implications for the woman writer include silence, double-voicedness, and challenge met with scorn.

The postcolonial dilemma of the African woman writer thus provides a valuable clue concerning Emecheta's textual ambivalence. Her "venturing into feminist consciousness," to borrow Nancy Topping Bazin's phrase, is a self-willed act that veils deep-seated fears about being disloyal to African culture.[34] This fact may account for her self-description as "an African feminist with a small f."[35] While the statement is a way of marking the psychological and cultural borders of her fiction, it is also a cautionary move, akin to the renunciation of the term by both Woolf and Drabble. Woolf's own fear of patriarchal retaliation has been noted by feminist critics. Jane Marcus, for example, describes her as "[a] guerrilla fighter in a Victorian skirt [who] trembled with fear as she prepared her attack, her raids on the enemy."[36] Fear underpins Woolf's obsessional practice of revision; her prolonged struggle with the angel in the house; her refusal, like Clarissa, to say, "I'm this or I'm that" (11); and ultimately her ambivalence regarding issues like race, class, and sexuality about which she was deeply concerned. Walker has also known fear. The world-weary women of her early fiction testify to an anxiety of status within not only gender and racial ideologies but also the African-American literary tradition. Walker, however, demonstrates in *The Color Purple* that feminism can be emboldened by the audacious womanist spirit.

Emecheta is poised to make the necessary creative adjustments. In *Destination Biafra* she seems to establish the groundwork for future artistic projects that will retrieve African femininity from the compromised space inscribed in *The Joys of Motherhood;* in *The Rape of Shavi* and *The Family* she broadens her creative boundaries to include the European Other and the Caribbean diaspora, respectively. Finally, in her latest novel, *Kehinde,* Emecheta and the African female subject that is her thematic preoccupation cross an important threshold: the self-fulfilled woman Nnu Ego prayed for has arrived and she is carrying very little emotional baggage. What Emecheta refers to as her "stubborn" Igbo personality may not translate into literary womanism, but it promises new ways of conceiving women.[37]

Conclusion

Race only posed itself as an urgent issue to me in the last couple of years. . . . I didn't feel the necessity of discussing race until I had moved myself out of a French poststructuralist orbit and began talking about American literary criticism.

Jane Gallop, "Criticizing Feminist Criticism"

By reading Woolf, Drabble, Emecheta, and Walker through the prism of womanism, I have tried both to provide a context for a theory of difference Walker advanced in 1983 and to rescue the term from its celebrants and detractors alike, relocating it in a neutral zone where it might begin to generate new critical energy. Walker's womanism is first and foremost a metaphor for feminism's continuing identity crisis. It points up the difficulty of theorizing femininity in the present poststructuralist culture. More crucially, womanism is a trope of otherness that facilitates an investigation of difference in the racialized zone of gender. Positing an oppositional black political aesthetic, Walker declared in 1983 open rebellion against the politics of exclusion that dominated white feminist praxis. Today, in a less confrontational climate, womanism makes for a sobering reading of difference, for the deepening not of the racial lines that divide women, but of the knowledge needed to better understand differences. The vitality of womanist critique thus lies in the opportunity it offers to probe the nature of the feminist project and the forces that promote and impede its goals.

Seizing this opportunity, I have isolated in this book what I consider to be a thoroughly womanist view and used it as a gauge for determining the validity of the claims it makes about itself and about white feminist literary practice. To read Woolf and Drabble through womanist eyes, as I have done, is to enact womanist theory's implicit "othering" of white feminism. The womanist mirror held up to Woolf and Drabble identifies distinctively areas of alignment and difference between the black and white feminist projects of liberation. I also read Walker against herself, revealing a map that is decidedly womanist-friendly in *The Color Purple* and at the same time shows deep fault-lines in her early fiction. Walker's construction of a homogeneous black feminist subject is shown to stand on tenuous, essentialist grounds not only through a reading of Emecheta but also of pre-womanist Walker.

Amid mounting concern about identity and difference within feminism, this probe of the limits and possibilities of Walker's theory leads inexorably to the question, what is the big promise of womanism? To begin, the womanist idea strikes at the heart of some of the basic issues in feminism. One of these is that the gendered ascendancy of white women in the women's movement of the 1960s gave rise to exclusionary practices that in turn engendered counter-ideas and practices, producing a climate of hostility and distrust. The growing presence and influence of the racial and cultural Other call for mapping new strategies to negotiate difference.

A fact brought out in this book by the intertextual reading of womanist theory is that difference also contains sameness, that boundaries (cultural, racial, or gendered) are dynamic and fluid. There is considerable slippage between the texts and authors, in spite of their material and ideological differences. They are linked by gender, the shared sense of commitment to social change, and by belief in the transformative power of art. There are other links as well, albeit tenuous: Walker has acknowledged a connection between Woolf's artistic projects and her own; Woolf is Drabble's literary mother; Walker is one of the earliest commentators of Emecheta's fiction and the first African American woman writer to recognize Emecheta's artistic potential; and finally, Emecheta's self-exile in England connects here to Woolf and Drabble.

Having established the relatedness of these writers, let us take a look at the present state of relations within feminism. A cursory look at the landscape will reveal the following picture: Western feminism is undergoing a cultural translation; women of color are breaking barriers across race, gender, and class; African American women writers have been restored to significance; and their Third World counterparts have taken their rightful place in feminism. However, beneath this placid exterior suspicions and anxiety continue to bubble over the question of power, for while white women continue to dominate the field and its discourses, emerging black and Third world communities now represent a strong political and intellectual force, fueling fears about shifts in power. This issue broke to the surface recently in a published conversation in which Jane Gallop made the admission cited in the epigraph.[1]

Gallop admitted to being too preoccupied in the mid- to late-eighties with male French theorists to notice the explosion of black women's writing and black feminist criticism that took place during the same period in the U.S. Ready now to focus attention on this body of work, Gallop admits to being as anxiety-ridden about encountering black feminist critics as she was about studying French poststructuralist theorists.

The ill-fated comparison Gallop makes between black feminist critics and French male theorists speaks to the fact that the hegemonic attitudes that engendered womanist theory are still in place, even if slightly altered. Where differences were ignored, they are now exaggerated, a concrete indication of the refusal to meet the racial Other on equal grounds. The question of encountering the Other underlies womanist intervention in feminist politics. Walker's conscious assertion of black feminist difference compels scrutiny of the white feminist Other. Ultimately, it is an effort to reach a level of understanding that will eliminate Gallop's or Spacks's anxiety of influence with relation to black/Third World feminist critics and writers.

To the extent that womanist theory enables the crossing of borders within racial gender, its utopian and essentialist shortcomings pale in comparison to its authorization of cultural and racial understandings in the Other-resistant terrain of feminism.

Notes

Introduction

1. Kate Millet, *Sexual Politics* (New York: Bantam Books, 1969).

2. For a trenchant analysis of the uneasy coexistence of the civil rights and women's movements in the 1960s, see Paula Giddings, *Where and When I Enter: The Impact of Black Women on Race and Sex in America* (New York: Bantam Books, 1984), 300–24.

3. Examples include: Shulamith Firestone, *Dialectic of Sex: The Case for Feminist Revolution* (New York: Bantam Books, 1970); Mary Daley, *Beyond God the Father: Toward a Philosophy of Women's Liberation* (Boston: Beacon Press, 1973); Dorothy Dinnerstein, *The Mermaid and the Minotaur: Sexual Arrangements and Human Malaise* (New York: Harper and Row, 1977); Nancy Chodorow, *The Reproduction of Mothering: Psychoanalysis and the Sociology of Gender* (Berkeley: University of California Press, 1978).

4. See, for example, Gloria T. Hull, Patricia Bell Scott, and Barbara Smith, eds., *But Some of Us Are Brave* (Old Westbury, NY: Feminist Press, 1982); Cherríe Moraga and Gloria Anzaldúa, eds., *This Bridge Called My Back: Writings by Radical Women of Color* (New York: Kitchen Table, Women of Color Press, 1983); Bonnie Thornton Dill, "Race, Class, and Gender: Prospects for an All-Inclusive Sisterhood," *Feminist Studies* 9 (Spring 1983): 131–50; Maria C. Lugones and Elizabeth V. Spelman, "Have We Got a Theory for You: Feminist Theory, Cultural Imperialism, and the Demand for 'The Woman's Voice'," *Women's Studies*, International Forum 6, no. 6 (1983): 573–81; Audre Lorde, "A Letter to Mary Daly," in *Sister Outsider* (Freedom, CA: The Crossing Press, 1984): 66–71; Elizabeth V. Spelman, *Inessential Woman: Problems of Exclusion in Feminist Thought* (Boston: Beacon Press, 1988).

5. Alice Walker, "One Child of One's Own: A Meaningful Digression Within the Work(s)," in *In Search of Our Mothers' Gardens: Womanist Prose by Alice Walker* (New York: Harcourt Brace Jovanovich, 1983), 372. Emphasis is Walker's. Ensuing parenthetical page references are to this text. Walker answers Spacks's question as follows: "Why only these? Because they are white and middle class, and because, to Spacks, female imagination is only that." She finishes off her rebuttal with a particularly poignant observation: ("Yet Spacks never lived in nineteenth-century Yorkshire, so why theorize about the Brontës?") See, also, Patricia Meyer Spacks, *The Female Imagination* (New York: Knopf, 1975) and Phyllis Chesler, *Women and Madness* (New York: Simon and Schuster, 1978).

6. Barbara Smith, "Towards a Black Feminist Criticism," in *The New Feminist Criticism*, ed. Elaine Showalter (New York: Pantheon Books, 1985), 171–72.

7. Calvin C. Hernton, *The Sexual Mountain and Black Women Writers: Adventures in Sex, Literature and Real Life* (New York: Anchor Press, 1987), 40.

8. Claudia Tate, "Reshuffling the Deck; Or, (Re)Reading Race and Gender in Black Women's Writing," *Tulsa Studies in Women's Literature* 7, no. 1 (Spring 1988): 128; Hernton, *The Sexual Mountain*, 47.

9. Tate, "Reshuffling the Deck," 128.

10. Smith, "Towards a Black Feminist Criticism," 174.

11. Mary Helen Washington, ed., *Black-Eyed Susans: Classic Stories By and About Black Women of Color* (Garden City: Anchor Books, 1975); *Midnight Birds: Stories by Contemporary Black Women Writers* (Garden City: Anchor·Books, 1980); *Invented Lives: Narratives of Black Women, 1860–1960* (Garden City: Doubleday, 1987); Henry Louis Gates, Jr., ed., *The Schomburg Library of Nineteenth-Century Black Women Writers* (New York: Oxford University Press, 1988). See, also, Roseann P. Bell, Bettye J. Parker, and Beverly Guy-Sheftall, eds., *Sturdy Black Bridges: Visions of Black Women in Literature* (Garden City: Anchor Books, 1979).

12. Deborah McDowell, "New Directions for Black Feminist Criticism," in *The New Feminist Criticism: Essays on Women, Literature and Theory*, ed. Elaine Showalter (New York: Pantheon Books, 1985), 186–99.

13. Hazel Carby, *Reconstructing Womanhood: The Emergence of the Afro-American Woman Novelist* (New York: Oxford University Press, 1987), 6.

14. Carby, *Reconstructing Womanhood*, 15.

15. Chikwenye Ogunyemi, "Womanism: The Dynamics of the Contemporary Black Female Novel in English," *Signs* 11, no. 1 (Autumn 1985): 63.

16. Ogunyemi, "Womanism," 64.

17. Ogunyemi, "Womanism," 71.

18. Barbara Smith, *Home Girls: A Black Feminist Anthology* (New York: Kitchen Press, 1983), xxiv.

19. Patricia Hill Collins, *Black Feminist Thought: Knowledge, Consciousness and the Politics of Empowerment* (Boston: Unwin Hyman, 1990), 39.

20. Clenora Hudson-Weems, *Africana Womanism: Reclaiming Ourselves* (Troy, MI: Bedford Publishers, 1993), 22. For perspectives on African feminism, see, for example, Filomena Chioma Steady, ed., *The Black Woman Cross-Culturally* (Cambridge, MA: Schenkman Publishing Co., 1988), 7–41; Molara Ogundipe-Leslie, "African Women, Culture and Another Development," *The Journal of African Marxists*, 5 (February 1984): 77–92; Carol Boyce Davies and Anne Adams Graves, eds., *Ngambika: Studies of Women in African Literature* (Trenton, NJ: Africa World Press, Inc., 1986); and my Afterword to Ama Ata Aidoo, *Changes* (New York: The Feminist Press, 1993), 171–96.

21. Hudson-Weems, *Africana Womanism*, 36.

22. Hudson-Weems, *Africana Womanism*, 21.

23. Carby, *Reconstructing Womanhood*, 16.

24. McDowell, "New Directions," 196.

25. Bell Hooks, *Talking Back: Thinking Feminist, Thinking Black* (Boston: South End Press, 1989), 181–82.

26. I use the term "mainstream" in this context advisedly. The truth of the matter is that while a small number of black feminist critics now command considerable attention within feminist discourse, neither they nor their work has attained the preeminence accorded Euro-American feminist ideas and their producers.

27. bell hooks, *Yearning: Race, Gender, and Cultural Politics* (Boston: South End Press, 1990), 28.

28. hooks, *Yearning*, 108. The "prescriptive" label is reminiscent of McDowell's "critical absolutism."

29. See Paule Marshall, *Brown Girl, Brownstones* (New York: Feminist Press, 1959), 102; Toni Morrison, *Sula* (New York: Bantam Books, 1975). For Sojourner Truth's "Ain't I a Woman" speech, see *Black Women in Nineteenth-Century American Life: Their Words, Their Thoughts, Their Feelings*, eds. Bert James Loewenberg and Ruth Bogin (Univer-

sity Park: The Pennsylvania State University Press, 1976), 235–36; Jacqueline Bernard, *Journey Toward Freedom: The Story of Sojourner Truth* (New York: Norton, 1967); Angela Davis, *Women, Race and Class* (New York: Vintage Books, 1983), 60–64. For an analysis of the defiant nature of Morrison's heroine and text, see Hortense Spillers's, "A Hateful Passion, A Lost Love," *Feminist Studies* 9, no. 2 (Summer 1983): 293–323.

30. Anna Julia Cooper, *A Voice from the South* (New York: Oxford University Press, 1988), 31.

31. Joyce Ladner, *Tomorrow's Tomorrow: The Black Woman* (New York: Anchor Books, 1971), 281.

32. Michael Awkward, *Inspiring Influences: Tradition, Revision, and Afro-American Women's Novels* (New York: Columbia University Press, 1989), 97.

33. W. E. B. DuBois, *The Souls of Black Folk* (New York: Vintage Books, 1990), 8.

34. Frantz Fanon, *The Wretched of the Earth* (New York: Grove Weidenfeld, 1963), 41.

35. Fanon, *Wretched*, 210, 215.

36. See Loewenberg and Bogin, eds., *Black Women in Nineteenth-Century American Life*, 274.

37. Cooper, *A Voice*, 120–25.

38. See Loewenberg and Bogin, eds., *Black Woman in Nineteenth-Century American Life*, 188–89.

39. Bessie Head, *A Woman Alone* (Portsmouth, NH: Heinemann, 1990), 99. For a distinction between black/Third World women's humanistic practices and western humanism, see *Third World Women and the Politics of Feminism*, eds. Chandra Talpade Mohanty, Ann Russo, and Lourdes Torres (Bloomington: Indiana University Press, 1973), 73.

40. Ann duCille, *The Coupling Convention: Sex, Text, and Tradition in Black Women's Fiction* (New York: Oxford University Press, 1993), 147. For a discussion of the speakerly text see, Henry Louis Gates, *The Signifying Monkey* (New York: Oxford University Press, 1988).

41. Walker in Agnes Smedley, *Daughter of Earth* (New York: The Feminist Press, 1987), 1. Emphasis is Walker's.

42. See, for example, "Saving the Life That Is Your Own: The Importance of Models in the Artist's Life" and "Beyond the Peacock: The Reconstruction of Flannery O'Connor" in *In Search of Our Mothers' Gardens*, 3–14; 42–59.

43. Rosemarie Tong, *Feminist Thought: A Comprehensive Introduction* (Boulder: Westview Press, 1989), 31.

44. Minrose C. Gwin, "A Theory of Black Women's Texts and White Women's Readings, or . . . The Necessity of Being Other," *National Women's Studies Association Journal*, 1, no. 1 (1988): 23.

45. Jane Marcus lends credence to the political rather than stylistic definition of aesthetics. See "Still Practice, A/Wrested Alphabet: Toward a Feminist Aesthetic," in *Feminist Issues in Literary Scholarship*, ed., Shari Benstock (Bloomington: Indiana University Press, 1987), 79.

Chapter 1

1.Woolf, *The Waves* (New York: Harcourt Brace Jovanovich, 1931), 76.

2. Berenice A. Carroll, "To Crush Him in Our Own Country: The Political Thought of Virginia Woolf," *Feminist Studies* 4, no. 1 (February 1978): 99–131. See, also, for example Naomi Black, "Virginia Woolf and the Women's Movement" in *Virginia Woolf: A Feminist Slant*, ed. Jane Marcus (Lincoln: University of Nebraska Press, 1983), 180–97; Brenda Silver, "*Three Guineas* Before and After: Further Answers to Correspondence," in *Virginia Woolf: A Feminist Slant*, 254–76; Susan M. Squier, *Virginia Woolf and London: Sexual Politics of the City* (Chapel Hill: University of North Carolina Press, 1985); Jane Marcus, "Britannia Rules *The Waves*" in *Decolonizing Tradition*, ed. Karen Lawrence (Urbana: University of Illinois Press, 1992): 136–61.

3. See, for example, Alex Zwerdling, *Virginia Woolf and the Real World* (Berkeley: University of California Press, 1986); Elaine Showalter, ed., *A Literature of Their Own: British Women Novelists from Brontë to Lessing* (Princeton: Princeton University Press, 1977); ensuing parenthetical page references are to this text; Bradford K. Mudge, "Burning Down the House: Sara Coleridge, Virginia Woolf, and The Politics of Literary Revision," *Tulsa Studies in Women's Literature* 5, no. 2 (Fall 1986): 229–50.

4. Woolf, "A Sketch of the Past," in *Moments of Being: Unpublished Autobiographical Writings*, Jeanne Schulkind, ed. (New York: Harcourt Brace Jovanovich, 1976), 65.

5. Woolf, *Moments of Being*, 18. For an insightful discussion of Woolf's notion of reality, see, Mark Hussey, *The Singing of the Real*

World: The Philosophy of Virginia Woolf's Fiction (Columbus: Ohio State University Press, 1986).

6. Winifred Holtby, *Virginia Woolf: A Critical Memoir* (Chicago: Academy Press, 1978) 24–25.

7. Margaret L. Davies, ed. *Life As We Have Known It* (New York: W. W. Norton, 1975), xxvi.

8. Woolf, *Moments of Being*, 182–98.

9. Woolf, *Three Guineas* (New York: Harcourt Brace Jovanovich, 1938), 107.

10. E. M. Forster, *Abinger Harvest* (New York: Harcourt Brace Jovanovich, 1936), 37.

11. Woolf, *A Room of One's Own*, (New York: Harcourt Brace Jovanovich, 1929), 52. Ensuing parenthetical page references are to this text.

12. Mark Hussey, *The Singing of the Real World: The Philosophy of Virginia Woolf's Fiction* (Columbus: The Ohio State University Press, 1986), 133.

13. Woolf, *The Voyage Out* (London: Hogarth, 1915), 336. Ensuing parenthetical page references are to this text.

14. Abdul JanMohamed, "The Economy of Manichean Allegory: The Function of Racial Difference in Colonialist Literature," in *"Race," Writing, and Difference*, ed., Henry Louis Gates, Jr. (Chicago: The University of Chicago Press, 1985), 84.

15. Toril Moi, *Sexual/Textual Politics* (New York: Methuen, 1985), 12.

16. Makiko Minow-Pinkney, *Virginia Woolf and the Problem of the Subject* (New Brunswick, NJ: Rutgers University Press, 1987), 3.

17. Woolf, "Women and Fiction," in *Granite and Rainbow* (New York: Harcourt Brace Jovanovich, 1958), 78.

18. Woolf, *A Writer's Diary* (New York: Harcourt Brace Jovanovich, 1953), 56. Ensuing parenthetical page references are to this text.

19. Woolf, *Mrs. Dalloway* (New York: Harcourt Brace Jovanovich, 1925), 154. Ensuing parenthetical page references are to this text.

20. Elaine Showalter, *Sexual Anarchy: Gender and Culture at the Fin de Siècle* (New York: Penguin Books, 1990) 127–43.

21. Woolf, *The Death of the Moth and Other Essays* (New York: Harcourt, Brace and Company, 1942), 174. Reading Conrad through the prism of postcolonial theory, Abdul JanMohamed broadly agrees with Woolf's assessment ("Forster does not present us with stereo-

types," he asserts), but his theoretical eye does not fail to see the ambiguities inherent in Forster's representation of the racial Other which he ascribes to the colonialist perception of the "native's inferiority as an unalterable metaphysical fact." See Abdul JanMohamed, "The Economy of Manichean Allegory: The Function of Racial Difference in Colonialist Literature," in *"Race," Writing, and Difference,* ed., Henry Louis Gates, Jr. (Chicago: The University of Chicago Press, 1985), 92–93.

22. Woolf, *Three Guineas,* 21, 97. Ensuing parenthetical page references are to this text.

23. Jenny Sharpe, *Allegories of Empire: The Figure of Woman in the Colonial Text* (Minneapolis: University of Minnesota, 1993), 92.

24. Susan M. Squier, *Virginia Woolf and London: Sexual Politics of the City* (Chapel Hill: University of North Carolina Press, 1985), 15.

25. See Edward Said, *Orientalism* (New York: Vintage Books/Random House, 1979); Said defines Orientalism "as a kind of Western projection onto and will to govern over the Orient," 95.

26. Sharpe, *Allegories of Empire: The Figure of Woman in the Colonial Text,* 57.

27. E. M. Forster, "Notes on the English Character," in *Abinger Harvest* (New York: Harcourt Brace Jovanovich, 1936), 10.

28. Margaret Drabble, *The Middle Ground,* (New York: Knopf, 1980), 243. Ensuing parenthetical page references are to this text.

29. Louise Bennett, "Colonization in Reverse," in *Breaklight: The Poetry of the Caribbean,* ed. Andrew Salkey (Garden City, NY: Doubleday, 1973), 51–52.

30. Forster, "Notes on the English Character," 5.

31. See for example Nupur Chaudhuri and Margaret Strobel, eds., *Western Women and Imperialism: Complicity and Resistance* (Bloomington: Indiana University Press, 1992).

32. Woolf's short fiction gives a fuller picture of her attitude toward the working class. See, for example, "The Journal of Mistress Joan Martyn," "The Shooting Party," and "The Mysterious Case of Miss V," in *The Complete Shorter Fiction of Virginia Woolf,* ed. Susan Dick (New York: Harcourt Brace Jovanovich, 1985).

33. Alex Zwerdling, "Mrs. Dalloway and the Social System," in *Mrs. Dalloway: Modern Critical Interpretations,* ed. Harold Bloom (New York: Chelsea House Publishers, 1988), 152.

34. Rachel Bowlby, *Virginia Woolf: Feminist Destinations* (New York: Blackwell, 1988), 86.

35. Davies, ed., *Life As We Have Known It,* xxvi, xxviii–xxix.

36. Jane Marcus, "Storming the Toolshed," *Signs* 7 (Spring 1982): 4–8.

37. Nancy K. Miller, "Emphasis Added: Plots and Plausibilities in Women's Fiction," in *The New Feminist Criticism: Essays on Women, Literature and Theory,* ed. Elaine Showalter (New York: Pantheon Books, 1985), 356.

38. Woolf, "Mr. Bennett and Mrs. Brown," in *Collected Essays,* ed. Leonard Woolf, (London, Hogarth, 1966–67), Vol. 2: 337.

39. Marianne DeKoven, "Gendered Doubleness and the 'Origins' of Modernist Form," *Tulsa Studies in Women's Literature,* 8, no. 1 (Spring 1989): 20.

40. Minow-Pinkney, *Virginia Woolf and the Problem of the Subject* (New Jersey: Rutgers University Press, 1987), 4.

Chapter 2

1. See Diana Cooper-Clark, "Margaret Drabble: A Cautious Feminist," *Atlantic Monthly* (November 1980): 72.

2. Gillian Geer, "Beyond Determinism: George Eliot and Virginia Woolf," in *Women Writing and Writing about Women,* ed. Mary Jacobus (New York: Barnes and Noble, 1979), 94.

3. See Margaret Drabble, "A Woman Writer," *Books* 11 (Spring 1973): 4–6.

4. See Bernard Bergonzi, "Margaret Drabble," in *Contemporary Novelists,* 2d ed., ed. James Vinson (New York: St. Martins, 1976), 373.

5. Simone de Beauvoir, *The Second Sex,* ed. and trans. H. M. Parshley, (New York: Knopf, 1962), 2: 249.

6. Peter Firchow, ed., *The Writer's Place: Interviews on the Literary Situation in Contemporary Britain* (Minneapolis: University of Minnesota Press, 1974), 107.

7. Drabble, *A Summer Bird-Cage* (New York: Belmont Books, 1985), 149. Ensuing parenthetical page references are to this text.

8. For Woolf's definition of the "Angel in the House," see "Professions for Women" in *Women and Writing,* ed. Michèle Barrett (New York: Harcourt Brace Jovanovich, 1979); for her discussion of androgyny, see *A Room of One's Own,* chapter 6.

9. Ellen Cronan Rose, *The Novels of Margaret Drabble* (New Jersey: Barnes and Noble, 1980), 3–4.

10. Margaret Drabble, *The Garrick Year* (London: Weidenfeld and

Nicholson, 1963), 238. Ensuing parenthetical page references are to this text.

11. Nora Forster Stovel, *Margaret Drabble*, Starmont Contemporary Writers Series, no. 2, ed. Dale Salwak (Mercer Island, CA: Starmont House, 1989), 47.

12. "Earth mother" is Stovel's phrase in *Margaret Drabble*, 55; Joanne V. Creighton comments on Sarah's rigidity in *Margaret Drabble*, Contemporary Writers Series, ed. Malcolm Bradbury and Christopher Bigsby (New York: Methuen, 1985), 50.

13. Margaret Drabble, *The Millstone* (London: Weidenfeld and Nicolson, 1965), 7, 199. Ensuing parenthetical page references are to this text.

14. Susan Spitzer, "Fantasy and Femaleness in Margaret Drabble's *The Millstone*," in *Critical Essays on Margaret Drabble*, ed. Ellen Cronan Rose (Boston: G. K. Hall, 1985), 92.

15. Creighton, *Margaret Drabble*, 65; Rose, *The Novels of Margaret Drabble*, 28.

16. The interview source is Mel Gussow, "Margaret Drabble: A Double Life," *New York Times Book Review*, 9 October 1977, 40–41; the "nose-in-the-washing-machine school" is Drabble quoted in Rosalind Miles, *The Fiction of Sex: Themes and Functions of Sex Difference in the Modern Novel* (London: Vision Press, 1974), 156.

17. Margaret Drabble, *Jerusalem the Golden* (New York: Belmont, 1971).

18. Drabble, *Arnold Bennett: A Biography* (New York: Knopf, 1974), 47.

19. Margaret Drabble, *The Needle's Eye* (New York: Knopf, 1972); *The Realms of Gold* (New York: Knopf, 1975); *The Ice Age* (New York: Knopf, 1977); *The Radiant Way* (Toronto: McClelland and Stewart, 1987). Ensuing parenthetical page references are to *The Ice Age*.

20. Sherry B. Ortner, "Is Female to Male as Nature is to Culture?" in *Women, Culture and Society*, ed. Michelle Zimbalist Rosaldo and Louise Lamphere (Stanford: Stanford University Press, 1974), 67–87.

21. Elizabeth Fox-Genovese, "The Ambiguities of Female Identity: A Reading of the Novels of Margaret Drabble," *Partisan Review* 46, no. 2 (1979): 235. For a defense of Drabble's portrayal of Alison, see Elaine Tuttle Hansen, "The Uses of Imagination: Margaret Drabble's *The Ice Age*" in *Critical Essays on Margaret Drabble*, ed. Ellen Cronan Rose, 164–68.

22. Rose, *The Novels of Margaret Drabble*, 123.

23. E. M. Forster, *Howard's End* (New York: Vintage Books, 1921), 186-87.

24. Nancy S. Hardin, "An Interview with Margaret Drabble," *Contemporary Literature* 14 (1973): 173-95.

25. Jane Campbell, "Reaching Outwards: Versions of Reality in *The Middle Ground*," *Journal of Narrative Technique* 14 (1984): 30.

26. Hardin, "An Interview with Margaret Drabble," 284, 289.

27. Barbara Milton, "Margaret Drabble: The Art of Fiction LXX," *The Paris Review* 20 (Fall-Winter 1978): 44.

28. Margaret Drabble, "How Not to Be Afraid of Virginia Woolf," *Ms.* (November 1972): 68-70.

29. Creighton, *Margaret Drabble*, 25.

30. Roberta Rubenstein, "From Detritus to Discovery: Margaret Drabble's *The Middle Ground*," *Journal of Narrative Technique* 14 (1984): 1.

31. Cooper-Clark, "Margaret Drabble: A Cautious Feminist," 70.

32. Patrick Brantlinger, "Victorians and Africans: The Genealogy of the Myth of the Dark Continent," *Critical Inquiry* 12 (Autumn 1985): 181.

33. The following passage from *Orlando* illustrates the extent to which Woolf was influenced by the prevailing Victorian ideologies of race: "For love, to which we may now return, has two faces; one white, the other black; two bodies; one smooth, the other hairy. It has two hands, two feet, two tails, two, indeed of every member and each one is the exact opposite of the other. Yet, so strictly are they joined together that you cannot separate them. In this case, Orlando's love began her flight towards him with her white face turned, and her smooth and lovely body outwards. Nearer and nearer she came wafting before her airs of pure delight. All of a sudden . . . she wheeled about, turned the other way round; showed herself black, hairy, brutish; and it was Lust the vulture, not Love, the Bird of Paradise, that flopped foully and disgustingly, upon his shoulder." See *Orlando* (New York: Penguin, 1946), 71.

Chapter 3

1. Alice Walker, *In Search of Our Mothers' Gardens: Womanist Prose by Alice Walker* (New York: Harcourt Brace Jovanovich, 1983), xi. The ensuing discussion of "womanishness" is based on this source; parenthetical page references are to this text.

2. Walker, *The Third Life of Grange Copeland* (New York: Harcourt

Brace Jovanovich, 1970), 4. Ensuing parenthetical page references are to this text.

3. Trudier Harris, "Violence in *The Third Life of Grange Copeland,*" *CLA Journal* 19 (1975): 239.

4. Bettye J. Parker-Smith, "Alice Walker's Women: In Search of Some Peace of Mind" in *Black Women Writers,* ed. Mari Evans (New York: Doubleday, 1983), 481.

5. Walker, *In Love & Trouble: Stories of Black Women* (New York: Harcourt Brace Jovanovich, 1973), 28. Ensuing parenthetical page references are to this text.

6. Mary Helen Washington, "Teaching *Black-Eyed Susans:* An Approach to the Study of Black Women Writers" in *But Some of Us Are Brave,* ed. Gloria T. Hull et al. (New York: The Feminist Press, 1982), 212.

7. Walker, *Meridian,* (New York: Harcourt Brace Jovanovich, 1976), 39. Ensuing parenthetical page references are to this text.

8. Walker's Saxon College recalls Naxos, the conservative black college in *Quicksand.* While the academic climate at Saxon is supportive, Helga Grane flees from the stifling bourgeois atmosphere at Naxos. See Nella Larsen, *Quicksand* (New Brunswick, NJ: Rutgers Unviersity Press, 1986).

9. Walker, *You Can't Keep a Good Woman Down* (New York: Harcourt Brace Jovanovich, 1981), 70.

10. Walker, "Saving the Life That Is Your Own: The Importance of Models in the Artist's Life" in *In Search of Our Mothers' Gardens,* 7.

11. Barbara Christian, "Alice Walker: The Black Woman Artist as Wayward" in *Black Feminist Criticism,* ed. Barbara Christian (New York: Pergamon Press, 1985), 83.

12. Walker, *Living by the Word: Selected Writings, 1973–1987* (New York: Harcourt Brace Jovanovich, 1988), 163–64. Ensuing parenthetical page references are to this text.

13. Felipe Smith provides an interesting perspective on this theme in "Alice Walker's Redemptive Art," *African American Review* 6, no. 3 (Fall 1992): 437–51.

14. Christine Froula, "The Daughter's Seduction: Sexual Violence and Literary History," in *Feminist Theory in Practice and Process,* ed. Micheline R. Malson et al. (Chicago: The University of Chicago Press, 1989), 155.

15. Froula, "The Daughter's Seduction," 161.

16. Walker, *The Color Purple* (New York: Washington Square Press, 1982), 30. Ensuing parenthetical page references are to this text.

17. For a discussion of Celie's survival capabilities, see Gina Michelle Collins, "*The Color Purple:* What Feminism Can Learn from a Southern Tradition," in *Southern Literature and Literary Tradition,* ed. Jefferson Humpheries (Athens: The University of Georgia Press, 1990), 75–87.

18. Hortense Spillers, "A Hateful Passion, A Lost Love," *Feminist Studies* 9, no. 2 (Summer 1983): 293–323.

19. I submit Shug to greater scrutiny in "Womanism Revisited: Women and the (Ab)use of Power in *The Color Purple.*" See *Feminist Nightmares: Women at Odds,* ed. Judith Fleischner and Susan Weisser (New York: New York University Press), 1994.

20. bell hooks, *Talking Back* (Boston: South End Press, 1989) 129.

21. Deborah K. King, "Multiple Jeopardy, Multiple Consciousness: The Context of a Black Feminist Ideology," in *Feminist Theory in Practice and Process,* ed. Micheline R. Malson et al., 91.

22. Froula, "The Daughter's Seduction," 159.

23. See Hazel Carby, *Reconstructing Womanhood: The Emergence of the Afro-American Woman Novelist* (New York: Oxford University Press, 1987), 95–175, and Sandra M. Gilbert and Susan Gubar, *The Madwoman in the Attic: The Woman Writer and the Nineteenth-Century Literary Imagination* (New Haven: Yale University Press, 1978).

24. Marilyn R. Farwell, "Toward a Definition of the Lesbian Literary Imagination," in *Feminist Theory in Practice and Process,* ed. Micheline R. Malson et al., 213.

25. Linda Alcoff, "Cultural Feminism versus Post-Structuralism: The Identity Crisis in Feminist Theory," in *Feminist Theory in Practice and Process,* ed. Malson et al., 308–9.

Chapter 4

1. See "A Writer Because of Not In Spite of, Her Children" in *In Search of Our Mothers' Gardens: Womanist Prose by Alice Walker* (New York: Harcourt Brace Jovanovich, 1983), 66–70. Walker praises Emecheta's ability to combine writing and mothering, a fact she believes Westerners, including herself, could benefit from.

2. Buchi Emecheta, *Head Above Water* (London: Fontana, 1986), 23.

3. Lloyd W. Brown, *Women Writers in Black Africa* (London: Greenwood Press, 1981), 35.

✓ 4. Emecheta, "Feminism With a Small 'f'!," in *Criticism and Ideology*, ed. Kirsten Holst Petersen, Second African Writers' Conference, Seminar Proceedings No. 20 (Uppsala: Scandinavian Institute of African Studies, 1988), 175.

5. Ngũgĩ wa Thiong'o *Decolonising the Mind: The Politics of Language in African Literature* (London: James Currey, 1987), 3.

6. For a discussion of the impasse between feminism and nationalist ideology, see my "Afterword" to Ama Ata Aidoo's novel *Changes* (New York: The Feminist Press, 1993).

✓ 7. Emecheta, "It's Me Who's Changed," *Connexions: An International Women's Quarterly* 4 (Spring 1982): 4–5.

8. *Emecheta, Head Above Water*, 29.

9. Chikwenye Ogunyemi, "Buchi Emecheta: The Shaping of a Self," *Komparatistiche Hefte* 8 (1983): 66; Brown, *Women Writers in Black Africa*, 48.

10. Emecheta, *Second Class Citizen* (New York: George Braziller, 1974), 69; emphasis added. Ensuing parenthetical page references are to this text.

11. Brown, *Women Writers in Black Africa*, 39.

12. Shoshana Felman, "Women and Madness: The Critical Phallacy," in *The Feminist Reader: Essays in Gender and the Politics of Literary Criticism*, ed. Catherine Belsey and Jane Moore (New York: Basil Blackwell, 1989), 34.

13. Emecheta, *The Bride Price* (New York: George Braziller, 1976), 168.

14. Emecheta, "It's Me Who's Changed," 5.

15. *The Slave Girl* is a fictional rendition of events in the life of Emecheta's mother; see *Head Above Water*, 6. Ensuing parenthetical page references to the novel are to *The Slave Girl* (New York: George Braziller, 1977).

16. Catherine Stimpson, "Gertrude Stein and the Transposition of Gender," in *The Poetics of Gender*, ed. Nancy K. Miller (New York: Columbia University Press, 1986), 4.

17. Emecheta, *The Joys of Motherhood* (New York: George Braziller, 1979), 8. Ensuing parenthetical page references are to this text.

18. Adrienne Rich, *Of Woman Born* (New York: W. W. Norton, 1986), 13.

19. Marie Umeh, "*The Joys of Motherhood:* Myth or Reality," *Colby Library Quarterly* 78 (1982): 39.

20. Katherine Frank, "The Death of the Slave Girl: African Womanhood in the Novels of Buchi Emecheta," *World Literature Written in English* 21 (1982): 478.

21. Eustace Palmer, "The Feminist Point of View: Buchi Emecheta's *The Joys of Motherhood,*" African Literature Today no. 13: *Recent Trends in the Novel,* ed. Eldred Durosimi Jones (New York: Africana Publishing, 1983), 39.

22. Stimpson, "Gertrude Stein and the Transposition of Gender," 10.

23. Deirdre David, *Intellectual Women and Victorian Patriarchy* (Ithaca, NY: Cornell University Press, 1987), 24.

24. Marianne DeKoven, "Gendered Doubleness and the 'Origins' of Modernist Form," *Tulsa Studies in Women's Literature* 8, no. 1 (Spring 1989): 36.

25. Felman, "Women and Madness." 134.

26. Emecheta, *Head Above Water,* 3.

27. Marianne DeKoven, "Gendered Doubleness," 36.

28. For a discussion of relations between colonizers and the colonized, see for example Franz Fanon, *Black Sin, White Masks,* trans. Charles Lam Markmann (New York: Grove Press, 1967); Patrick Brantlinger, *Rule of Darkness: British Literature and Imperialism, 1830–1914* (Ithaca, NY: Cornell University Press, 1988); O. Mannoni, *Prospero and Caliban: The Psychology of Colonization,* trans. Pamela Powersland (Ann Arbor: University of Michigan Press, 1990).

29. Emecheta, "Feminism With a Small 'f'!," 75.

30. wa Thiong'o, "The Canon in Africa: Imperialism and Racism," in *The Informed Reader,* ed. Charles Bazerman (New York: Houghton Mifflin, 1989), 60. See *Writers in Politics,* (London: Heinemann, 1981).

31. wa Thiong'o, *Decolonising the Mind: The Politics of Language in African Literature* (London: James Currey, 1987), 93.

32. Chinweizu et al., *Toward the Decolonization of African Literature, African Fiction and Poetry and Their Critics,* Vol. 1 (Washington, DC: Howard Unversity Press, 1983), 5.

33. Adeola James, ed., *In Their Own Voices: African Women Writers Talk,* Studies in African Literature (London: James Currey, 1990), 67.

34. Nancy Topping Bazin, "Venturing Into Feminist Consciousness: Two Protagonists from the Fiction of Buchi Emecheta and Bessie Head," *Sage* Vol. II, no. 1 (Spring 1985), 32.

35. Emecheta, "Feminism With a Small 'f'!," 175.

36. Jane Marcus, *Art & Anger: Reading Like a Woman* (Columbus: Ohio University Press, 1988), 73.

37. "I think the Igbos are very stubborn. If I want to drink from this cup and someone says, 'no', I just have to do it. It is that or nothing," Emecheta tells Adeola James in an interview in *In Their Own Voices: African Women Writers Talk* (London: James Currey, 1990), 32.

Conclusion

1. Jane Gallop, Marianne Hirsch, Nancy K. Miller, "Criticizing Feminist Criticism," in *Conflicts in Feminism,* ed. Marianne Hirsch and Evelyn Fox Keller (New York: Routledge, 1990), 363.

Bibliography

Abel, Elizabeth, Marianne Hirsch, and Elizabeth Langland. *The Voyage In: Fictions of Female Development.* Hanover, NH: University Press of New England, 1983.

Aidoo, Ama Ata. *Changes.* New York: The Feminist Press, 1993.

Alcoff, Linda. "Cultural Feminism versus Post-Structuralism: The Identity Crisis in Feminist Theory." In *Feminist Theory in Practice and Process,* eds. Micheline R. Malson et al. Chicago: The University of Chicago Press, 1989.

Allan, Tuzyline Jita. "Womanism Revisited: Women and the (Ab)use of Power in *The Color Purple.*" In *Feminist Nightmares: Women at Odds,* eds. Judith Fleischner and Susan Weisser. New York: New York University Press, 1994.

Ashcroft, Bill, Gareth Griffiths, and Helen Tiffin. *The Empire Writes Back: Theory and Practice in Post-Colonial Literatures.* London: Routledge, 1989.

Awkward, Michael. *Inspiriting Influences: Tradition, Revision, and Afro-American Women's Novels.* New York: Columbia University Press, 1989.

Baker, Houston A., Jr. *Workings of the Spirit: The Poetics of Afro-American Women's Writing.* Chicago: The University of Chicago Press, 1991.

Barrett, Michèle, ed. *Women and Writing.* New York: Harcourt Brace Jovanovich, 1979.

Batchelor, John. *Virginia Woolf: The Major Novels.* Cambridge: Cambridge University Press, 1991.

Bazerman, Charles, ed. *The Informed Reader.* New York: Houghton Mifflin, 1989.

Beards, Virginia. "Margaret Drabble: Novels of a Cautious Feminist." *Critique* 15 (1973): 35–47.

Bell, Roseann P. "The Absence of the African Woman Writer." *CLA Journal* 21, no. 4 (1978): 491.

Bell, Roseann P., Bettye J. Parker, and Beverly Guy-Sheftall, eds. *Sturdy Black Bridges: Visions of Black Women in Literature.* Garden City: Anchor Books, 1979.

Benhabib, Seyla, and Drucilla Cornell, eds. *Feminism As Critique: On the Politics of Gender.* Minneapolis: University of Minnesota Press, 1987.

Bennett, Louise. "Colonization in Reverse." In *Breaklight: The Poetry of the Caribbean,* ed. Andrew Salkey (Garden City, NY: Doubleday, 1973).

Benstock, Shari, ed. *Feminist Issues in Literary Scholarship.* Bloomington: Indiana University Press, 1987.

Bergonzi, Bernard. "Margaret Drabble." In *Contemporary Novelists,* ed. James Vinson. New York: St. Martins, 1976.

Bernard, Jacqueline. *Journey Toward Freedom: The Story of Sojourner Truth.* New York: Norton, 1967.

Black, Naomi. "Virginia Woolf and the Women's Movement." In *Virginia Woolf: A Feminist Slant,* ed. Jane Marcus. Lincoln: University of Nebraska Press, 1983.

Bloom, Harold, ed. *Mrs. Dalloway: Modern Critical Interpretations.* New York: Chelsea House Publishers, 1988.

Bornstein, George, ed. *Representing Modernist Texts: Editing as Interpretation.* Ann Arbor: University of Michigan Press, 1991.

Bowlby, Rachel. *Virginia Woolf: Feminist Destinations.* New York: Blackwell, 1988.

Bradbury, Malcolm. *The Modern World: Ten Great Writers.* New York: Penguin Books, 1988.

Brantlinger, Patrick. *Rule of Darkness: British Literature and Imperialism, 1830–1914.* Ithaca, NY: Cornell University Press, 1988.

———. "Victorians and Africans: The Genealogy of the Myth of the Dark Continent." *Critical Inquiry* 12 (Autumn 1985): 166–203.

Brown, Lloyd W. *Women Writers in Black Africa.* London: Greenwood Press, 1981.

Campbell, Jane. "Reaching Outwards: Versions of Reality in *The Middle Ground.*" *Journal of Narrative Technique* 14 (1984): 17–32.

Carby, Hazel. *Reconstructing Womanhood: The Emergence of the Afro-American Woman Novelist.* New York: Oxford University Press, 1987.

Carroll, Berenice A. "To Crush Him in Our Own Country: The Political Thought of Virginia Woolf." *Feminist Studies* 4, no. 1 (February 1978): 99–131.

Chaudhuri, Nupur, and Margaret Strobel, eds. *Western Women and Imperialism: Complicity and Resistance.* Bloomington: Indiana University Press, 1992.

Chesler, Phyllis. *Women and Madness.* New York: Simon and Schuster, 1978.

Childers, Mary and Bell Hooks. "A Conversation About Race and Class." In *Conflicts in Feminism,* eds. Marianne Hirsch and Evelyn Fox Keller. New York: Routledge, 1990.

Chodorow, Nancy. *The Reproduction of Mothering: Psychoanalysis and the Sociology of Gender.* Berkeley: University of California Press, 1978.

Christian, Barbara, ed. *Black Feminist Criticism.* New York: Pergamon Press, 1985.

Cohen, Ralph, ed. *The Future of Literary Theory.* New York: Routledge, Chapman & Hall, 1989.

Collins, Gina Michelle. "*The Color Purple:* What Feminism Can Learn from a Southern Tradition." In *Southern Literature and Literary Tradition,* ed. Jefferson Humpheries. Athens: The University of Georgia Press, 1990.

Collins, Patricia Hill. *Black Feminist Thought: Knowledge, Consciousness and the Politics of Empowerment.* Boston: Unwin Hyman, 1990.

Cooper, Anna Julia. *A Voice from the South.* New York: Oxford University Press, 1988.

Cooper-Clark, Diana. "Margaret Drabble: A Cautious Feminist." *Atlantic Monthly* (November 1980): 69–75.

Creighton, Joanne V. *Margaret Drabble,* eds. Malcolm Bradbury and Christopher Bigsby. New York: Methuen, 1985.

Daley, Mary. *Beyond God the Father: Toward a Philosophy of Women's Liberation.* Boston: Beacon Press, 1973

David, Deirdre. *Intellectual Women and Victorian Patriarchy.* Ithaca, NY: Cornell University Press, 1987.

Davies, Carole Boyce, and Anne Adams Graves, eds. *Ngambika: Studies of Women in African Literature.* Trenton, NJ: Africa World Press, 1986.

Davies, Margaret L., ed. *Life As We Have Known It.* New York: W. W. Norton, 1975.

Davis, Angela. *Women, Race and Class.* New York: Vintage Books, 1983.

de Beauvoir, Simone. *The Second Sex*, trans. and ed. H. M. Parshley. New York: Knopf, 1962.

DeKoven, Marianne. "Gendered Doubleness and the 'Origins' of Modernist Form." *Tulsa Studies in Women's Literature* 8, no. 1 (Spring 1989): 19–42.

Dill, Bonnie Thornton. "Race, Class, and Gender: Prospects for an All-Inclusive Sisterhood." *Feminist Studies* 9 (Spring 1983): 131–50.

Dinnerstein, Dorothy. *The Mermaid and the Minotaur: Sexual Arrangements and Human Malaise.* New York: Harper and Row, 1977.

Donaldson, Laura E. *Decolonizing Feminisms: Race, Gender, and Empire-building.* Chapel Hill: The University of North Carolina Press, 1992.

Drabble, Margaret. "A Woman Writer," *Books* 11 (Spring 1973): 4–6.

———. *Arnold Bennett: A Biography.* New York: Knopf, 1974.

———. *The Garrick Year.* London: Weidenfeld and Nicholson, 1963.

———. "How Not to Be Afraid of Virginia Woolf." *Ms* (November 1972): 68–70.

———. *The Ice Age.* New York: Alfred A. Knopf, 1977.

———. *Jerusalem the Golden.* New York: Belmont, 1971.

———. *The Middle Ground.* New York: Knopf, 1980.

———. *The Millstone.* London, Weidenfeld & Nicolson, 1965.

———. *The Needle's Eye.* New York: Knopf, 1972.

———. *The Radiant Way.* Toronto: McClelland and Stewart, 1987.

———. *The Realms of Gold.* New York: Knopf, 1975.

———. *A Summer Bird-Cage.* New York: Belmont Books, 1985.

DuBois, W. E. B. *The Souls of Black Folk.* New York: Vintage Books, 1990.

duCille, Ann. *The Coupling Convention: Sex, Text, and Tradition in Black Women's Fiction.* New York: Oxford University Press, 1993.

Eisenstein, Hester, and Alice Jardine, eds. *The Future of Difference.* New Brunswick, NJ: Rutgers University Press, 1988.

Emecheta, Buchi. *The Bride Price.* New York: George Braziller, 1976.

———. *Destination Biafra.* London: Allison and Busby Ltd., 1982.

———. "Feminism With a Small 'f'!." In *Criticism and Ideology,* ed. Kirsten Holst Petersen. Uppsala: Scandinavian Institute of African Studies, 1988.

———. *Head Above Water.* London: Fontana, 1986.

———. *In the Ditch.* London: Barrie and Jenkins, 1972.

———. "It's Me Who's Changed." *Connexions: An International Women's Quarterly* 4 (Spring 1982): 4–5.

_____. *The Joys of Motherhood.* New York: George Braziller, 1979.

_____. *Second Class Citizen.* New York: George Braziller, 1974.

_____. *The Slave Girl.* New York: George Braziller, 1977.

Evans, Mari. *Black Women Writers (1950–1980): A Critical Evaluation.* New York: Anchor Books/Doubleday, 1984.

Fanon, Frantz. *Black Skin, White Masks,* trans. Charles Lam Markmann. New York: Grove Press, 1967.

_____. *The Wretched of the Earth.* New York: Grove Weidenfeld, 1963.

Farwell, Marilyn R. "Toward a Definition of the Lesbian Literary Imagination." In *Feminist Theory in Practice and Process,* eds. Micheline R. Malson et al. Chicago: The University of Chicago Press, 1989.

Felman, Shoshana. "Women and Madness: The Critical Phallacy." In *The Feminist Reader: Essays in Gender and the Politics of Literary Criticism,* eds. Catherine Belsey and Jane Moore. New York: Basil Blackwell, 1989.

Felski, Rita. *Beyond Feminist Aesthetics: Feminist Literature and Social Change.* Cambridge: Harvard University Press, 1989.

Firchow, Peter, ed. *The Writer's Place: Interviews on the Literary Situations in Contemporary Britain.* Minneapolis: University of Minnesota Press, 1974.

Firestone, Shulamith. *Dialectic of Sex: The Case for Feminist Revolution.* New York: Bantam Books, 1970

Fleischner, Judith and Susan Weisser, eds. *Feminist Nightmares: Women at Odds.* New York: New York University Press, 1994.

Forster, E. M. *Abinger Harvest.* New York: Harcourt Brace Jovanvich, 1936.

_____. *Howard's End.* New York: Vintage Books, 1921.

Fox-Genovese, Elizabeth. "The Ambiguities of Female Identity: A Reading of the Novels of Margaret Drabble." *Partisan Review,* 46, no. 2 (1979): 234–48.

Frank, Katherine. "The Death of the Slave Girl: African Womanhood in the Novels of Buchi Emecheta." *World Literature Written in English.* 21 (1982): 476–97.

Froula, Christine. "The Daughter's Seduction: Sexual Violence and Literary History." In *Feminist Theory in Practice and Process,* eds. Micheline R. Malson et al. Chicago: The University of Chicago Press, 1989.

Fuss, Diana. *Essentially Speaking: Feminism, Nature and Difference.* New York: Routledge, Chapman & Hall, 1989.

Gallop, Jane. *Around 1981: Academic Feminist Literary Theory.* New York: Routledge, Chapman & Hall, 1992.

Gallop, Jane, Marianne Hirsch, and Nancy K. Miller. "Criticizing Feminist Criticism." In *Conflicts in Feminism,* eds. Marianne Hirsch and Evelyn Fox Keller. New York: Routledge, 1990.

Gates, Henry Louis, Jr., ed. *"Race," Writing, and Difference.* Chicago: The University of Chicago Press, 1985.

———. *Reading Black, Reading Feminist: A Critical Anthology.* New York: Meridian, 1990.

———. *The Schomburg Library of Nineteenth-Century Black Women Writers.* New York: Oxford University Press, 1988.

———. *The Signifying Monkey.* New York: Oxford University Press, 1988.

Gates, Henry Louis, Jr., and K. Anthony Appiah. *Alice Walker: Critical Perspectives Past and Present.* New York: Amistad Press, 1993.

Greer, Gillian. "Beyond Determinism: George Eliot and Virginia Woolf." In *Women Writing and Writing about Women,* ed. Mary Jacobus. New York: Barnes and Noble, 1979.

Giddings, Paula. *Where and When I Enter: The Impact of Black Women on Race and Sex in America.* New York: Bantam Books, 1984.

Gilbert, Sandra M. and Susan Gubar. *The Madwoman in the Attic: The Woman Writer and the Nineteenth-Century Literary Imagination.* New Haven: Yale University Press, 1978.

Greene, Gayle, and Coppélia Kahn, eds. *Making a Difference: Feminist Literary Criticism.* London: Methuen & Co., 1986.

Gussow, Mel. "Margaret Drabble: A Double Life." *New York Times Book Review,* 9 October 1977, 40–41.

Gwin, Minrose C. "A Theory of Black Women's Texts and White Women's Readings, or . . . The Necessity of Being Other." *National Women's Studies Association Journal,* 1, no. 1 (1988): 23.

Hansen, Elaine Tuttle. "The Uses of Imagination: Margaret Drabble's *The Ice Age.*" In *Critical Essays on Margaret Drabble,* ed. Ellen Cronan Rose. Boston: G. K. Hall, 1985.

Hardin, Nancy S. "An Interview with Margaret Drabble." *Contemporary Literature* 14 (1973): 173–95.

Harris, Trudier. "Violence in *The Third Life of Grange Copeland.*" *CLA Journal* 19 (1975): 238–47.

Head, Bessie. *Maru.* African and Caribbean Writers Series. London: Heinemann, 1987.

———. *A Woman Alone.* Portsmouth, NH: Heinemann, 1990.

Hernton, Calvin C. *The Sexual Mountain and Black Women Writers: Adventures in Sex, Literature and Real Life.* New York: Anchor Press, 1987.

Hirsch, Marianne and Evelyn Fox Keller, eds. *Conflicts in Feminism.* New York: Routledge, 1990.

Holtby, Winifred. *Virginia Woolf: A Critical Memoir.* Chicago: Academy Press Limited, 1978.

Homans, Margaret. *Bearing the Word: Language and Female Experience in Nineteenth-Century Women's Writing.* Chicago: The University of Chicago Press, 1986.

hooks, bell. *Talking Back: Thinking Feminist, Thinking Black.* Boston: South End Press, 1989.

————. *Yearning: Race, Gender, and Cultural Politics.* Boston: South End Press, 1990.

Hudson-Weems, Clenora. *Africana Womanism: Reclaiming Ourselves.* Troy, MI: Bedford Publishers, 1993.

Hull, Gloria T., Patricia Bell Scott, and Barbara Smith, eds. *But Some of Us Are Brave.* Old Westbury, NY: Feminist Press, 1982.

Humpheries, Jefferson, ed. *Southern Literature and Literary Tradition.* Athens: The University of Georgia Press, 1990.

Hussey, Mark. *The Singing of the Real World: The Philosophy of Virginia Woolf's Fiction.* Columbus: Ohio State University Press, 1986.

Jacobus, Mary, ed. *Women Writing and Writing about Women.* New York: Barnes and Noble, 1979.

James, Adeola, ed. *In Their Own Voices: African Women Writers Talk.* Studies in African Literature. London: James Currey, 1990.

JanMohamed, Abdul. "The Economy of Manichean Allegory: The Function of Racial Difference in Colonialist Literature." In *"Race," Writing, and Difference,* ed. Henry Louis Gates, Jr. Chicago: The University of Chicago Press, 1985.

Kenyon, Olga. *Women Writers Talk.* New York: Carroll & Graf Publishers, 1990.

King, Deborah K. "Multiple Jeopardy, Multiple Consciousness: The Context of a Black Feminist Ideology." In *Feminist Theory in Practice and Process,* eds. Micheline R. Malson et al. Chicago: The University of Chicago Press, 1989.

Ladner, Joyce A. *Tomorrow's Tomorrow: The Black Woman.* New York: Anchor Books/Doubleday, 1971.

Larsen, Nella. *Quicksand.* New Brunswick, NJ: Rutgers Unviersity Press, 1986.

Lawrence, Karen, ed. *Decolonizing Tradition*. Urbana: University of Illinois Press, 1992.

Loewenberg, Bert James and Ruth Bogin, eds. *Black Women in Nineteenth-Century American Life: Their Words, Their Thoughts, Their Feelings*. University Park: The Pennsylvania State University Press, 1976.

Lorde, Audre. *Sister Outsider*. Freedom, CA: The Crossing Press, 1984.

Lugones, Maria C. and Elizabeth V. Spelman. "Have We Got a Theory for You: Feminist Theory, Cultural Imperialism, and the Demand for The Woman's Voice'." *Women's Studies International Forum* 6, no. 6 (1983): 573–81.

McDowell, Deborah. "New Directions for Black Feminist Criticism." In *The New Feminist Criticism: Essays on Women, Literature and Theory*, ed. Elaine Showalter. New York: Pantheon Books, 1985.

Malson, Micheline R. et al., eds. *Feminist Theory in Practice and Process*. Chicago: The University of Chicago Press, 1989.

Mannoni, O. *Prospero and Caliban: The Psychology of Colonization*, trans. Pamela Powersland. Ann Arbor: University of Michigan Press, 1990.

Marcus, Jane. *Art & Anger: Reading Like a Woman*. Columbus: Ohio University Press, 1988.

——. "Britannia Rules *The Waves*." In *Decolonizing Tradition*, ed. Karen Lawrence. Urbana: University of Illinois Press, 1992.

——. "Still Practice, A/Wrested Alphabet: Toward a Feminist Aesthetic." In *Feminist Issues in Literary Scholarship*, ed. Shari Benstock. Bloomington: Indiana University Press, 1987.

——. "Storming the Toolshed." *Signs* 7 (Spring 1982): 4–80.

Marcus, Jane, ed. *Virginia Woolf: A Feminist Slant*. Lincoln: University of Nebraska Press, 1983.

Marshall, Paule. *Brown Girl, Brownstones*. New York: Feminist Press, 1959.

Miles, Rosalind. *The Fiction of Sex: Themes and Functions of Sex Difference in the Modern Novel*. London: Vision Press, 1974.

Miller, Nancy K., ed. *The Poetics of Gender*. New York: Columbia University Press, 1986.

Millet, Kate. *Sexual Politics*. New York: Bantam Books, 1969.

Milton, Barbara. "Margaret Drabble: The Art of Fiction LXX." *The Paris Review* 20 (Fall-Winter 1978): 40–65.

Minow-Pinkney, Makiko. *Virginia Woolf and the Problem of the Subject*. New Brunswick, NJ: Rutgers University Press, 1987.

Mohanty, Chandra Talpade, Ann Russo, and Lourdes Torres, eds.

Third World Women and the Politics of Feminism. Bloomington: Indiana University Press, 1973.

Moi, Toril. *Sexual/ Textual Politics.* New York: Methuen, 1985.

Moraga, Cherríe and Gloria Anzaldúa, eds. *This Bridge Called My Back: Writings by Radical Women of Color.* New York: Kitchen Table, Women of Color Press, 1983.

Morrison, Toni. *Sula.* New York: Bantam Books, 1975.

Mudge, Bradford K. "Burning Down the House: Sara Coleridge, Virginia Woolf, and The Politics of Literary Revision." *Tulsa Studies in Women's Literature* 5, no. 2 (Fall 1986): 229–50.

Ngcobo, Lauretta. "African Motherhood—Myth and Reality." In *Criticism and Ideology,* ed. Kirsten Holst Petersen. Uppsala: Scandinavian Institute of African Studies, 1988.

Ogundipe-Leslie, Molara. "African Women, Culture and Another Development." *The Journal of African Marxists,* 5 (February 1984): 77–92.

Ogungemi, Chikwenye. "Buchi Emecheta: The Shaping of a Self." *Komparatistiche Hefte* 8 (1983): 65–78.

_____. "Womanism: The Dynamics of the Contemporary Black Female Novel in English," *Signs* 11, no. 1 (Autumn 1985): 63.

Ortner, Sherry B. "Is Female to Male as Nature is to Culture?" In *Women, Culture and Society,* eds. Michelle Zimbalist Rosaldo and Louise Lamphere. Stanford: Stanford University Press, 1974.

Palmer, Eustace. "The Feminist Point of View: Buchi Emecheta's *The Joys of Motherhood." African Literature Today,* no. 13, 1983.

Parker-Smith, Bettye J. "Alice Walker's Women: In Search of Some Peace of Mind." In *Black Women Writers,* ed. Mari Evans. New York: Doubleday, 1983.

Petersen, Kirsten Holst, ed. *Criticism and Ideology.* Uppsala: Scandinavian Institute of African Studies, 1988.

Rich, Adrienne. *Of Woman Born.* New York: W. W. Norton, 1986.

_____. *On Lies, Secrets, and Silence: Selected Prose 1966–1978.* New York: W. W. Norton, 1979.

Robinson, Sally. *Engendering the Subject: Gender and Self-Representation in Contemporary Women's Fiction.* Albany: State University of New York at Albany Press, 1991.

Rosaldo, Michelle Zimbalist and Louise Lamphere, Eds. *Women, Culture and Society.* Stanford: Stanford University Press, 1974.

Rose, Ellen Cronan, ed. *Critical Essays on Margaret Drabble.* Boston: G. K. Hall, 1985.

————. "Margaret Drabble: Surviving the Future." *Critique* 15 (1973): 5–21.

————. *The Novels of Margaret Drabble*. New Jersey: Barnes and Noble, 1980.

Rosser, Sue Vilhauer. *Biology and Feminism: A Dynamic Interaction*. New York: Twayne Publishers, 1992.

Rubenstein, Roberta. "From Detritus to Discovery: Margaret Drabble's *The Middle Ground*." *Journal of Narrative Technique* 14 (1984): 1–16.

Said, Edward. *Orientalism*. New York: Vintage Books/Random House, 1979.

Schipper, Mineke. "Mother Africa on a Pedestal: The Male Heritage in African Literature and Criticism." *Women in African Literature Today*, no. 15, 1987.

Sharpe, Jenny. *Allegories of Empire: The Figure of Woman in the Colonial Text*. Minneapolis: University of Minnesota Press, 1993.

Showalter, Elaine. *A Literature of Their Own: British Women Novelists from Brontë to Lessing*. Princeton: Princeton University Press, 1977.

————. *The New Feminist Criticism*. New York: Pantheon Books, 1985.

————. *Sexual Anarchy: Gender and Culture at the Fin de Siècle*. New York: Penguin Books, 1990.

Silver, Brenda. "*Three Guineas* Before and After: Further Answers to Correspondence." In *Virginia Woolf: A Feminist Slant*, ed, Jane Marcus. Lincoln: University of Nebraska Press, 1983.

Smedley, Agnes. *Daughter of Earth*. New York: The Feminist Press, 1987.

Smith, Barbara. *Home Girls: A Black Feminist Anthology*. New York: Kitchen Press, 1983.

————. "Towards a Black Feminist Criticism." In *The New Feminist Criticism*, ed. Elaine Showalter. New York: Pantheon Books, 1985.

Smith, Felipe. "Alice Walker's Redemptive Art," *African American Review* 6, no. 3 (Fall 1992): 437–51.

Spacks, Patricia Meyer. *The Female Imagination*. New York: Knopf, 1975.

Spelman, Elizabeth V. *Inessential Woman: Problems of Exclusion in Feminist Thought*. Boston: Beacon Press, 1988.

Spillers, Hortense. "A Hateful Passion, A Lost Love." *Feminist Studies* 9, no. 2 (Summer 1983): 293–323.

Spitzer, Susan. "Fantasy and Femaleness in Margaret Drabble's *The*

Millstone." In *Critical Essays on Margaret Drabble,* ed. Ellen Cronan
Rose. Boston: G. K. Hall, 1985.

Sprinker, Michael, ed. *Edward Said: A Critical Reader.* Cambridge,
MA: Blackwell Publishers, 1992.

Squier, Susan M. *Virginia Woolf and London: Sexual Politics of the City.*
Chapel Hill: The University of North Carolina Press, 1985.

Steady, Filomina Chioma, ed. *The Black Woman Cross-Culturally.* Cambridge, MA: Schenkman Publishing Co., 1988.

Stimpson, Catherine. "Gertrude Stein and the Transposition of
Gender." In *The Poetics of Gender,* ed. Nancy K. Miller. New York:
Columbia University Press, 1986.

Stovel, Nora Forster. *Margaret Drabble.* Mercer Island, CA: Starmont
House, 1989.

Tate, Claudia, ed. *Black Women Writers at Work.* New York: Continuum
Publishing, 1984.

————. "Reshuffling the Deck; Or, (Re)Reading Race and Gender
in Black Women's Writing." *Tulsa Studies in Women's Literature* 7,
no. 1 (Spring 1988): 128.

Todd, Janet M. *Feminist Literary History.* New York: Routledge, Chapman & Hall, 1988.

Tong, Rosemarie. *Feminist Thought: A Comprehensive Introduction.* Boulder:
Westview Press, 1989.

Umeh, Marie. "*The Joys of Motherhood:* Myth or Reality." *Colby Library
Quarterly* 78 (1982): 39–46.

Vinson, James, ed. *Contemporary Novelists,* 2d ed. New York: St.
Martins, 1976.

wa Thiong'o, Ngũgĩ. "The Canon in Africa: Imperialism and
Racism." In *The Informed Reader,* ed. Charles Bazerman. New
York: Houghton Mifflin, 1989.

————. *Decolonising the Mind: The Politics of Language in African Literature.*
London: James Currey, 1987.

Walker, Alice. *The Color Purple.* New York: Washington Square Press,
1982.

————. *In Love & Trouble.* New York: Harcourt Brace Jovanovich,
1973.

————. *In Search of Our Mothers' Gardens: Womanist Prose by Alice Walker.*
New York: Harcourt Brace Jovanovich, 1983.

————. *Living by the Word: Selected Writings, 1973–1987.* New York:
Harcourt Brace Jovanovich, 1988.

————. *Meridian.* New York: Harcourt Brace Jovanovich, 1976.

_____. *In Search of Our Mothers' Gardens: Womanist Prose by Alice Walker.* New York: Harcourt Brace Jovanovich, 1983.

_____. *The Third Life of Grange Copeland.* New York: Harcourt Brace Jovanovich, 1970.

_____. *You Can't Keep a Good Woman Down.* New York: Harcourt Brace Jovanovich, 1981.

Washington, Mary Helen, ed. *Black-Eyed Susans: Classic Stories By and About Black Women of Color.* Garden City: Anchor Books, 1975.

_____. *Midnight Birds: Stories by Contemporary Black Women Writers.* Garden City: Anchor Books, 1980.

_____. *Invented Lives: Narratives of Black Women, 1860–1960.* Garden City: Doubleday, 1987.

_____. "Teaching *Black-Eyed Susans:* An Approach to the Study of Black Women Writers." In *But Some of Us Are Brave,* eds. Gloria T. Hull et al. New York: The Feminist Press, 1982.

Woolf, Virginia. *Collected Essays,* ed. Leonard Woolf. 4 vols. London, Hogarth, 1966–67.

_____. *The Complete Shorter Fiction of Virginia Woolf,* ed. Susan Dick. New York: Harcourt Brace Jovanovich, 1985.

_____. *The Death of the Moth and Other Essays.* New York: Harcourt, Brace and Company, 1942.

_____. *Granite and Rainbow.* New York: Harcourt Brace Jovanovich, 1958.

_____. *Moments of Being: Unpublished Autobiographical Writings,* ed. Jeanne Schulkind. New York: Harcourt Brace Jovanovich, 1976.

_____. *Mrs. Dalloway.* New York: Harcourt Brace Jovanovich, 1925.

_____. *Orlando.* New York: Penguin, 1946.

_____. *A Room of One's Own.* New York: Harcourt Brace Jovanovich, 1929.

_____. *Three Guineas.* New York: Harcourt Brace Jovanovich, 1938.

_____. *The Voyage Out.* London: Hogarth, 1915.

_____. *A Writer's Diary.* New York: Harcourt Brace Jovanovich, 1953.

_____. *The Waves: The Two Holograph Drafts.* Edited by J. W. Graham. Toronto: The University of Toronto Press, 1976.

Zwerdling, Alex. "Mrs. Dalloway and the Social System." In *Mrs. Dalloway: Modern Critical Interpretations,* ed. Harold Bloom. New York: Chelsea House Publishers, 1988.

_____. *Virginia Woolf and the Real World.* Berkeley: University of California Press, 1986.

Index

Achebe, Chinua, 103
Aesthetics, 98, 126; definition of,
    17; n. 45 126; Drabblean, 52;
    Emecheta's, 96–98; Walker's,
    75; Woolf's, 23, 64
Alcoff, Linda, 93
Austen, Jane, 64
Awkward, Michael, 12

Bazin, Nancy Topping, 116
Bennett, Arnold, 23–24, 38, 51, 64
Bennett, Louise, 31
Black Arts Movement, 10
Black feminist criticism, 5; devel-
    opment of, 4
Black feminist critics, 4–5, 9–10,
    n. 26 124
Black womanhood, 15, 75–76,
    100; construction of, 11;
    Walker's trajectory of, 75
Bowlby, Rachel, 35
Brantlinger, Patrick, 67
Brontë, Charlotte, 3, 38
Brown, Lloyd, 96, 100
Browning, Elizabeth Barrett, 106

Carby, Hazel, 5, 93
Camus, Albert, 76
Chesler, Phyllis, 2
Childers, Mary, 19
Chopin, Kate, 106
Christian, Barbara, 5, 81
Civil rights movement, 1, 78

Class, 2, 13, 21, 24, 50, 53, 93, 113,
    117, 120; and womanist
    ideology, 83; classism, 70;
    difference, 31; in *Mrs. Dalloway*,
    31–44; Woolf's politics of,
    15–16
Collins, Patricia Hill, 8
Colonial myths, 97
Colonialism, 83
Colonialist discourse, 22
Colonization, in *Mrs. Dalloway*, 25
Colonized, Other, 67
Conrad, Joseph, 22
Cooper, Anna Julia, 8

David, Deirdre, 106
de Beauvoir, Simone, 39, 47, 129
DeKoven, Marianne, 38, 44,
    106–7, 112
Determinism, 45; sexual, 47
Difference, sexual, 89; Woolf's
    representation of, 25, 28
Dinnerstein, Dorothy, 122
Drabble, Margaret, 16, 31, 45–47,
    49–60, 64, 67–68, 70, 96–97,
    120; *A Summer Bird-Cage*, 48;
    Jerusalem the Golden, 51, 62; *The
    Garrick Year*, 48, 64; *The Middle
    Ground*, 15–16, 31, 45–47, 51,
    53–55, 57–60, 65, 68, 70; *The
    Millstone*, 50; *The Needle's Eye*,
    51; *The Radiant Way*, 51; *The*

Realms of Gold, 51, 62; *The Waterfall,* 52, 64
DuBois, W. E. B., 12
duCille, Ann, 14

Eliot, George, 106
Emecheta, Buchi, 16–17, 94–104, 106–7, 109, 111–12, 114, 116, 120; *Destination Biafra,* 117; *In the Ditch,* 98–99, 101; *Second Class Citizen,* 95, 97–98, 101; *The Bride Price,* 100–2, 104; *The Family,* 117; *The Joys of Motherhood,* 15–16, 95, 98, 100, 104–17; *The Rape of Shavi,* 117; *The Slave Girl,* 100, 102
Essentialism, 15
Ethnocentrism, 2

Fanon, Frantz, 12
Fate, 43, 46, 48, 52, 58–60, 84, 89, 101, 105; sexual, 48, 52
Faulkner, William, 76, 81
Felman, Shoshana, 100, 110
Feminism, 3, 6, 11, 17, 19–20, 24, 37, 41, 60–61, 66–68, 92, 97–98, 106, 117–21; African, 8; black, 8; culture-specific, 8; dilemma of, 46; liberal, 15, 20, 70; second wave, 3; white, 3, 8–9, 70, 119; womanist intervention in, 54. *See also,* womanism
Feminist criticism, 2, 37; black, 4–5, 9–10, 120; white, 5, 17
Forster, E. M., 21
Fox-Genovese, Elizabeth, 52
Frank, Katherine, 106
Froula, Christine, 83

Gallop, Jane, 118, 120–21
Galsworthy, John, 24
Gates, Henry Louis, 4
Gender, 7, 11, 16–17, 20, 101, 106, 117, 119–20; and difference, 118; in African women's writings, 116; in Drabble, 46–47, 50, 53, 64; in Emecheta, 101; in Woolf, 23; racial, 3, 15, 121

Genet, Jean, 1
Gilbert, Sandra, 93
Gilman, Charlotte Perkins, 106
Greer, Gillian, 47
Griottes, 95
Gubar, Susan, 93
Gwin, Minrose, 17

Harris, Trudier, 71
Head, Bessie, 13
Hernton, Calvin, 3–4
Homans, Margaret, 37
hooks, bell, 9–10, 88
Hudson-Weems, Clenora, 8–9
Humanism, 12
Hurston, Zora Neale, 81
Hussey, Mark, 22

Identity, 3, 5, 14, 19, 23, 25, 41, 58, 79, 87, 99, 110, 116; African female, 116; black female, 11–12, 72–73; crisis in feminism, 118–19; Drabble's biodeterministic model of, 16–17, 49–52
Imperialism, 3, 24–27, 29, 115–16; and patriarchy, 33; critique of, 25

JanMohamed, Abdul, 22, 127 n. 21
Jordan, June, 8

Kristeva, Julia, 23

Ladner, Joyce, 11, 100, 125
Lawrence, D. H., 1
Lesbianism, 40, 43, 85
Lorde, Audre, 69, 122

Mailer, Norman, 1
Mallarmé, Stéphane, 17
Marcus, Jane, 37, 117
Marshall, Paule, 11
Martineau, Harriet, 106
McDowell, Deborah, 5
Miller, Henry, 1
Miller, Nancy K., 37
Millet, Kate, 1

Milton, Barbara, 59
Minow-Pinkney, Makiko, 23, 37
Modernism, 41; Woolf's, 23
Moi, Toril, 23
Morrison, Toni, 11, 26, 81
Motherhood, 77; black, 78; in *The Joys of Motherhood*, 104

Nationalism, 97; and feminism, 134
Ngcobo, Lauretta, 95

O'Connor, Flannery, 14–15, 76, 81
Ogundipe-Leslie, Molara, ix, 116
Ogunyemi, Chikwenye, 7, 98
Oppression, 11–12, 19–20, 23, 39, 70, 83, 89, 98, 110; patriarchal, 20; Woolf's knowledge of, 23
Ortner, Sherry B., 51

Palmer, Eustace, 106
Pan-Africanism, 7
Parker-Smith, Bettye, 71
Patriarchy, 6, 9, 15–16, 24–25, 29, 37, 39, 40, 42–43, 48, 64, 92, 97, 99, 102, 106; and African nationalism, 97; and white liberal feminism, 15; British women and, 3; feminist resistance to, 6; in "A Society," 39; in "A Woman's College from Outside," 40; in *Mrs. Dalloway*, 25, 42, 43; origin of, 37
Patriotism, 33, 40; in *Three Guineas*, 40
Phallocentrism, 2
Politics, of division, 9; of identity, 17; of inclusion, 13; of representation, 17
Postcolonial, and African literary discourse, 115; dilemma of the African woman writer, 116; reality of border crossings, 55
Predestination, 59; in Drabble, 59

Race, 17, 44, 59, 88, 92–93, 100, 116–17, 120; and womanism, 7–14, 16–17, 83; in contemporary London, 54; in *The Middle Ground*, 53–57; Victorian ideologies of, 131 n. 33
Racial, Other, 22, 29, 98, 119–20
Racism, 8, 70–72, 75, 96, 98, 115
Realism, Arnoldian, 41
Representation, 53
Rich, Adrienne, 45, 105
Rose, Ellen Cronan, 48, 53
Rubenstein, Roberta, 65

Sexism, 3, 70–72, 75, 98
Shakespeare, 7, 33, 36
Sharpe, Jenny, 27–29
Showalter, Elaine, 23
Simpson, Catherine, 106
Smedley, Agnes, 14, 93
Smith, Barbara, 3, 5, 7
Solipsism, 76
Spacks, Patricia Meyer, 2–3, 121
Spitzer, Susan, 50, 130
Squier, Susan, ix, 27
Stein, Gertrude, 44, 106
Stewart, Maria, 13
Stimpson, Catharine, 103, 106
Stovel, Nora Forster, 49

Tate, Claudia, 4
Things Fall Apart, 103
Thiong'o, Ngũgĩ wa, 97, 115–16
Truth, Sojourner, 11–12

Umeh, Marie, 106

Walker, Alice, 2–3, 5–10, 13–17, 20–21, 67–72, 74–77, 80–83, 88–90, 92–97, 99, 106, 118–20; *In Love & Trouble*, 71, 72–76, 80; *In Search of Our Mothers' Gardens*, 3, 6–7, 11, 71–72, 74–77, 81–82, 92, 95; *Meridian*, 77–80, 86–87, 93, 132; *The Color Purple*, 15–16, 68–71, 75–78, 80–81, 83–96, 106, 110, 113–15, 117, 119; *The Third Life of Grange Cope-*

land, 71, 72, 75–76; *You Can't
Keep a Good Woman Down,* 80
Washington, Mary Helen, 4,
    74–75
Wilde, Oscar, 17
Williams, Fannie Barrier, 12–13
Wollstonecraft, Mary, 66
Woman-centeredness, 6, 11–12, 20,
    37, 70
Womanist, 1, 4–17, 20, 54, 60, 67,
    69, 70, 74, 76, 83, 88, 90–99,
    101, 103–4, 106, 113, 117,
    119, 120–21; Africana wom-
    anism, 8; consciousness, 6;
    ideology, 83; themes, 6;
    theory, 9–10, 14–15, 119–21;
    womanish, 10; womanism,

5–11, 13–17, 69–70, 91–93,
    96, 98, 106, 117–19
Woolf, Virginia, 14–17, 19–27,
    29–35, 37–41, 43–46, 48,
    56–58, 64–65, 67–68, 70, 87,
    96–98, 116–17, 120; "A So-
    ciety," 38–41; "A Woman's
    College from Outside,"
    40–41, 43; *A Room of One's
    Own,* 21, 28, 37–38, 40–41, 45,
    64, 66–67, 127, 129; *Mrs. Dal-
    loway,* 15–16, 19, 20, 24, 26,
    29, 31, 34, 38, 41, 43–44, 46,
    53, 65, 67, 70, 85, 97, 113; *The
    Voyage Out,* 22; *The Waves,* 19;
    Three Guineas, 30, 37, 40, 45,
    67; *To the Lighthouse,* 42, 113

A Note about the Author

Tuzyline Jita Allan teaches in the English Department at Baruch College (CUNY). She is co-editor of *Literature Around the Globe* and has written several articles on twentieth-century women writers. She is currently working on a book about African women and nationalism.